LIFE UNDER
NAZI
OCCUPATION

LIFE UNDER
NAZI
OCCUPATION

THE STRUGGLE TO SURVIVE DURING
WORLD WAR II

PAUL ROLAND

Acknowledgements

The author wishes to express his gratitude to the following for providing archival material and sourcing academic publications – Michael Roland (Head Researcher) and Dany Deville. Also thank you to the following for indicating secondary sources: George Fotakis of Crete, Nikola Stojanovic, Jan Bogucki, Karen Swartz, RS Romain, Jeremy Chateau and Stig Slatuun.

Thank you also to Barbara Eldridge of the Anne Frank Fonds for permission to quote extracts from Anne Frank's diary ©ANNE FRANK FONDS Basel, Switzerland.

This edition published in 2020 by Arcturus Publishing Limited
26/27 Bickels Yard, 151–153 Bermondsey Street,
London SE1 3HA

AD006663UK

Printed in the UK

CONTENTS

CONTENTS

INTRODUCTION

'When diplomacy ends, war begins.'
Adolf Hitler

Adolf Hitler had envisaged establishing by force a New Order in Europe, which Germany would govern with an iron fist. Conceived as the natural successor to the Holy Roman Empire of 800–1806 and the German Empire of 1871–1918, the Third Reich would last a thousand years, would leave imposing ruins to compare with those of ancient Rome and would make either subjects or slaves of all the nations of Europe. Hitler believed himself to have been chosen by Providence to lead 'the revolutionary struggle' against Bolshevism and to raise a defeated and humiliated nation from its knees and urge it on to glory.

In speech after speech, he repeated his assertion that he had been entrusted with a quasi-religious mission, that of ridding the continent of 'inferior' races and of establishing the Germans and their Aryan brothers as the Master Race. No sacrifice would be too great to attain this end; no suffering would be too much to ask. And if the *Untermenschen*, or subhuman races, were eradicated in the process, then so be it. They were expendable.

Alliances would be made and promises broken with impunity. The end would justify the means. The *Übermenschen* – superior men – would not be restrained by laws, morality or religious dictates. National Socialism was the new religion, a pseudo-pagan cult with Hitler as its figurehead, *Mein Kampf* as its bible and the swastika supplanting the Christian cross.

Once the tanks were rolling across Europe's borders, the Führer's enemies routed, their cities reduced to rubble, German troops would march in triumph through the streets, fulfilling their destiny. All would be humbled and bow before them.

Adolf Hitler believed the Third Reich would last a thousand years and would leave imposing ruins to compare with those of ancient Rome. More than that, he wanted to make subjects or slaves of all the other nations of Europe.

This was a despot's dream, the febrile vision of a megalomaniac, but few in Germany, or in Hitler's native Austria, could see the abyss to which he was leading them. As Chancellor, he had done so much in a short time to restore German pride. As for his threats to eradicate the communists, the Jews and 'the undesirables', this was surely only rhetoric to whip up support among those who blamed Germany's enemies for their defeat in 1918. These 'excesses' would be curtailed in time and moderation would prevail.

The 'old enemy', France, and its allies, Britain and America, dreaded the thought of another war. They were weary after fighting the last one, which they had prayed would be 'the war to end wars', and were all too eager to secure peace at any price. Britain had its appeasers and America its isolationists and at the time of the 'Munich crisis' in September 1938, it seemed that their fear of another war might force them to come to an accommodation with Herr Hitler who, in defiance of the Versailles Treaty, had rearmed Germany and seemed in unseemly haste to put its new weapons, air force and highly disciplined troops to the test.

Too few had read *Mein Kampf*, in which the former corporal in the Bavarian army made no secret of his plans to conquer Eastern Europe, enslave the Slavs and implement the 'Final Solution' to the problem posed by the Jews: the persistent, pernicious myth that they exercised undue influence in world affairs to the detriment of hard-working, God-fearing Aryans.

The Nazis imposed laws and decrees on the conquered people of Europe that denied them their rights under international law, specifically the Hague Conventions of 1899 and 1907. The law of military occupation as defined in the Conventions does not grant the invader unlimited power over the population and yet, the Nazis, together with their Axis allies and various puppet regimes, deprived the conquered people of their security and protection to which they were entitled in time of war.

But the Nazis were inconsistent in their treatment of their occupied territories across Europe. They initially treated Nordic nations with some degree of sympathy and even consideration, in the hope that they might persuade the Danes, the Norwegians and the Dutch to join their mythical crusade against 'inferior' races. Meanwhile, the countries of Eastern Europe were to be Germanized by the forced eviction of the indigenous people and the settlement of German colonists. Denmark, Norway and Holland were to be assimilated into the Reich, while France was to become a German dependency. Poland and its neighbours were to be erased from the map, their property and businesses requisitioned and resources plundered.

In the first year of the occupation (1940–41), the Nazis issued many of the 330 decrees that were later collected in Raphael Lemkin's *Axis Rule In Occupied Europe* (1944), a damning indictment of Nazi policies which would be cited by war crimes investigators and the Allied occupation forces in post-war Europe. These reveal the contradictions and indecision that beset the regime, which had no co-ordinated policy in many significant areas and seemed to have been concocted from Hitler's informal 'table talks'. The Nazi leadership was deliberately vague when it came to describing the nature of their envisaged empire. Speaking to German newspapermen in April 1940, Propaganda Minister Joseph Goebbels said, 'If anyone asks how you conceive the new Europe, we have to reply that we don't know... When the time comes, we will know very well what we want.'

But a lack of unity and vision within the Nazi leadership would lead to confusion and a fierce, destructive rivalry. In their arrogance and naivety, Nazi party officials and department heads assumed that those in the occupied countries would accept the invasion of their territories and the displacement of their people without putting up a fight. But almost everywhere resistance was fierce and came from the most unlikely quarters. Ultimately, the will to survive while retaining some semblance of dignity and individuality proved the most potent force in the face of Nazi oppression.

CHAPTER 1
PRELUDE TO WAR

Occupation of the Rhineland – 7 March 1936

It could be argued that the German occupation of Europe began on 7 March 1936, for on that day German troops reoccupied the Rhineland in open defiance of both the Versailles Treaty and the Locarno Pact which guaranteed the borders of sovereign states.

This 30-mile (50 km) demilitarized strip along the Rhine bordering Germany and its old enemies France, Belgium and the Netherlands had been intended as a buffer zone to deter any future invasion by a belligerent and vengeful Germany. But Hitler was determined to demonstrate his disregard for the punitive restraints imposed on his country by the Allies after Germany's defeat in 1918 and also to establish his authority before a sceptical High Command which resented taking orders from the former corporal.

It was an audacious gamble. Had the French soldiers forced the Germans back, Hitler would have been humiliated, his plans for invading Europe postponed, or even abandoned. There was also a distinct possibility that disaffected members of the German General Staff might have been sufficiently emboldened to attempt a coup.

Unbeknown to the Allies, Hitler had issued an order that his troops were to withdraw if they encountered resistance. But the French failed to act, restrained by timid politicians who feared defeat at forthcoming elections if they advocated a conflict with Germany.

Britain too ignored Hitler's flagrant violation of the Versailles Treaty and justified its appeasement policy by claiming, in the words of Lord Lothian, that Germany was only 'walking into its own backyard'.

This conspicuous lack of initiative fatally weakened the League of Nations and it offered the Germans an opportunity to fortify the remilitarized zone, to the extent that the Siegfried line, as it was to be known, became a formidable barrier to be breached at war's end.

AUSTRIA and the Victim Myth – 12 March 1938

When the Allies occupied Vienna at the end of April 1945, they were greeted with a familiar plea heard in towns, cities and villages across Austria: 'Tommy, me no Nazi' and 'Down with Hitler' – this from the same people who had welcomed Hitler in March 1938 with tears of joy and hoarse cries of '*Sieg Heil*'.

A significant proportion of Austrians absolved themselves of any complicity in the crimes perpetrated by the Nazis by claiming to be victims of German aggression, a plea which fell on deaf ears, but which they clung to in their defence as fervently as a drowning man clings to a lifebelt. This myth of Austria as victim has persisted to this day.

However, at the time of Hitler's triumphant return to his birthplace, there were dissenting voices that were drowned out by the exultant mob. They were the voices of those Austrians who had not put a cross on their ballot paper during the recent plebiscite that legitimized the Anschluss, the annexation of Austria to the Greater German Reich. Moreover, these were neither Jews nor communists, but 'ordinary' men and women who were not enthralled by Hitler's charisma, nor were they persuaded by his promises to make them masters of the world. Their rejection of the Anschluss had been wilfully disregarded during the plebiscite when Nazi vote-riggers destroyed any ballot papers that did not endorse Hitler's mandate, an accusation substantiated by the fact that several districts recorded more than 100 per cent in favour.

A workforce subdued

On 26 March 1938, *Time* magazine published a report by an anonymous correspondent who witnessed the Nazi takeover of Vienna and its violent aftermath. He noted the doubt and anxiety expressed by those Austrians who felt they were now prisoners of an occupying force. They were to be found among the 'organized workers' (i.e. the trade unions), Catholics, Monarchists and 'liberal-minded non-political people of every sort'.

More than 100,000 Nazi storm troopers marched into Austria in March 1938, many singing patriotic songs, and this is a cross-section of the crowd that greeted them in the centre of Vienna. Gershon Evan, a Jew whose parents were murdered, said: 'What happened in Germany over five years happened in Vienna in five days. We had no idea we would face such violence.'

All were silenced by the display of Nazi power: the flight of bombers which circled the city at low altitude to intimidate those who might have been contemplating some form of resistance, the relentless parade of military might which coursed through the streets – lorries loaded with troops, gun carriages and tanks – and the deployment of armed soldiers to factories to coerce workers into remaining at their machines. These were the very same workers who only days before had sung the *Internationale* at numerous public meetings to protest against the imminent takeover of their country, which had proudly declared itself neutral and independent after the First World War.

But the 'Aryan middle-classes and lumpenproletariat', as the *Time* correspondent called them, had been seduced en masse. For so long, these citizens of a 'small but defenceless country' had looked on enviously as their German cousins proclaimed themselves the Master Race, their young men strutting and preening in their smart black uniforms and polished jackboots, cowing all Europe with their threatening presence. Now they were invited to join the proceedings, the Austrians succumbed to a form of mass hysteria, which overcame all rational thought.

'Hundreds', according to the correspondent, had already made an end to their own lives which had become 'intolerable and insane' and, he predicted, 'an equally horrible fate awaits the known leaders of the workers.'

The coming of war

The majority of Austrians may have greeted their most infamous son as a returning hero, but there was a sizeable opposition in the capital to the Nazis from the Social Democrats, who saw themselves as victims of tyranny. The Social Democratic labour movement in Vienna had been the largest in Europe during the 1920s, so much so that the capital had been commonly referred to as Red Vienna. Two out of every three voters had backed the Social Democrats and one in every three was a paid-up member of the party.

In addition, the Nazis faced vociferous opposition from the Catholic Church and its archly conservative members who were particularly strong and influential in Austria. So when Hitler annexed his birthplace, he knew he would have to suppress a significant portion of the population.

Cardinal Innitzer may have received Hitler with cordiality in public and ordered the ringing of the cathedral bells in honour of his return, but in private, the cardinal shared his reservations with his sister, who made her objections known in public.

More significantly, there were signs that the initial euphoria was swiftly evaporating, to be replaced by cynicism and disillusionment.

When the Nazis commandeered the best hotels and made free with whatever they felt was their due plunder, some of those who had been in favour of the Anschluss began to wonder if they might have made a mistake. As *Time* reported:

> One saw every evidence that the Germans considered them-selves the masters of a conquered country [...] Austrians had ceased to have any say in their own affairs [...] The German army, the German police, the German S.S., the German politi-cians [...] were running the place.

Time continued, 'There were already signs that in more than one section of the population doubts were beginning to insinuate themselves.' The reporter heard 'ordinary people' expressing their fears that war was not far off, that Vienna was already a city under siege and that the destruction that would befall Austria would be nothing compared to the stigma that would taint it for aligning itself with the National Socialist regime.

> One could only have imagined that the front was a few dozen miles away, and that war was already raging. And if one did know, there was only one thought possible—when will it begin?

Insulting the Führer

The summer of 1938 saw the resurgence of the communists who issued anti-Nazi pamphlets and on every vacant wall posted fly-sheets and scrawled graffiti accusing the National Socialists of reneging on their promises. Unemployment had actually risen in rural areas and no investment had been made in Austria's ailing industries. Regular work and higher wages were only offered to those willing to work in Germany, where the foreign workers' presence was resented by their German co-workers. Those who had work and remained in Austria began to notice that their wage packets were lighter, due to the imposition of higher German taxes.

Within a year of the Anschluss, Gestapo agents were reporting a worrying increase in anti-Nazi sentiments being expressed openly in bars and cafés, much of it criticism of Hitler, who was accused of favouring his adopted fatherland at the expense of his birthplace. They even had a new category of offence to cover it, the so-called *Führerbeleidigung* (insulting the Führer). Most of the criticism was of the familiar type aimed at politicians by disaffected voters, but some of it came from former acquaintances, or those claiming to have known Hitler in his Vienna days, accusing the Führer of disreputable behaviour and habits – which the Gestapo could not allow to go unpunished.

A former classmate, an unnamed woman from Fischlham, told anyone who would listen, 'He was always a crook, even as a ten-year-old. And more than anything, he liked torturing animals.' She was hauled into a Nazi court, convicted of insulting the Führer and sentenced to six months in prison. Her sentence was reported in the Austrian press as a warning to others, but the offending words she was accused of uttering were omitted from the reports.

Others held their tongues until the failed assassination attempt on the Führer in November 1939 prompted some to express the wish that the bomber had succeeded and more than one offer to do the job properly.

Hostility to war

When war came, the Austrians reacted with weary scepticism. Absenteeism rose dramatically and with it a significant drop in production. It was widely believed that a fall-off in production would mean that the war would end sooner.

The War Economy Decrees were seen as a burden imposed on a recalcitrant population who had no desire to be allies in Hitler's war and bitterly resented having to send their young men to fight on the Eastern Front, just as they had done in 1914. They were openly hostile to the swarms of unskilled Russian women and the Polish POWs who had been sent to work in the factories and fields and who required feeding and housing when both resources were already stretched to the limit.

Defeatism sets in

Cynicism, particularly among the Viennese, expressed itself in many forms, including open defiance of authority and there were even isolated acts of sabotage. As Tim Kirk notes in his *History Today* article, 'Workers and Nazis In Hitler's Homeland', 'Colliding trains and burning haystacks were a weekly event in wartime Austria.'

Desperate Viennese Jews stand in line in 1938 waiting to obtain a visa for Poland. These people were frightened, but few could imagine the hellish consequences if they failed to leave the Austrian capital.

News of Germany's invasion of Russia in June 1941 brought evidence of open support for the Russians, not only among Austria's communists, but also from those who secretly hoped it would be the undoing of 'the little corporal' who had finally overreached himself.

With the defeat at Stalingrad in February 1943, a turning point in German–Austrian relations was reached. Many Austrians believed the rumours that their compatriots had taken the brunt of the beating meted out to the Sixth Army on the Volga. It was widely rumoured that Austria's young men had been deliberately sacrificed to give the Sixth Army more time to regroup and make a last stand after Hitler had refused them permission to retreat.

Now seeing themselves as 'second-class Germans', or the Greater Reich's provincial cousins, defeatism set in. As Tim Kirk notes, 'There was no national resistance, but, apart from the weeks after the Anschluss, there was no convincingly national acclamation of Hitler either... the Austrians were too busy picking their way to work through the rubble to give coherent expression to their disgruntlement with the war and with the regime.'

Coming home to die

Despite Austria being annexed rather than occupied, there were thousands of Austrian citizens who suffered under Nazi tyranny in their own country, some of whom committed suicide after the war because they felt unable to live with the memory of what they had endured.

In Austria, during the war, the non-Jewish partners of mixed marriages lived a precarious existence. Constantly under the threat of deportation, they were never quite sure which of the discriminatory laws applied to them, nor when minor transgressions might result in their imprisonment or death. They were ostracized by Austrian society and shunned by orthodox Jews while attempting to maintain secular lives and protect their families.

One Catholic woman, Mathilde Hahn, bore the burden of providing for her Jewish husband and their children at a time when she, as for the majority of women, was expected to be a full-time mother or *Hausfrau*. A few years after the war, she committed suicide, worn out by the strain and the 'degradation' of living what amounted to a lie.

Others were driven to despair through forced conscription into labour units such as those of Organization Todt (OT), where thuggish, convicted criminals presided over the conscripted – and sometimes abducted – slave workforce. Spouses of Jews were among those drafted for work; according to historian Michaela Raggam-Blesch of Vienna University, 'There are indications that this [forced conscription] was intended to disrupt these families and to impair the protection of "Aryan" spouses in order to facilitate future deportations.' One such spouse was Oskar Baader, a veteran of the First World War. Having been deprived of his livelihood as a schoolteacher by the Nazis solely because he had married a Jewess, in the last months of the war, he had been drafted into the OT forced labour unit on the Hungarian border. As a result of his suffering there, in November 1945, he took his own life. According to his son, he had returned to Vienna to die.

Even before the Nazis marched into Austria, Oskar had learned what National Socialism would mean for those who shared Hitler's nationality and religion, but who had 'stained' their Aryan origins by marrying a Jew. He was refused membership of the German Academic Anglicist Association even though he had yet to marry his fiancée. Consequently, he was forced to abandon his plans for an academic career. Instead, he took a job as a high school teacher, with poorer prospects and lower pay.

When the Nazis entered Vienna, the whole catalogue of anti-Jewish laws sanctioned by the Reichstag became Austrian law with immediate effect. Jewish spouses of Aryan partners were not subject to the degrading treatment meted out to their Jewish married neighbours; they were not called upon, for example, by the 'cleaning squads', who forced Jews to scrub the streets to the evident amusement of jeering mobs. But they were acutely aware that they were now subject to the odious Nuremberg Laws of September 1935 which made them third-class citizens in their own country.

Intermarried families were considered an affront to Nazi ideology and the racial origin of the Jewish spouse was deemed to be unchanged by their marriage, leaving them open to persecution and imprisonment under those same laws.

The authorities put pressure on the non-Jewish partner to petition for divorce and offered all sorts of enticements to persuade them to do so. Some relented and lived with the guilt and shame to the end of their days. Others did so willingly and, in doing so, became unwitting collaborators.

Those who refused were dismissed from their jobs and forced to find other temporary and insecure employment. Oskar Baader gave private lessons and supplemented his meagre income from the pension to which he was still entitled. Those who owned businesses were forcibly deprived of them and others had their shops and factories vandalized. Families were then entirely dependent on income earned by their Aryan spouses or their grown-up children.

Their situation was made even more precarious when it meant being evicted from their homes, as happened to those who lived in community housing.

The Nazis in Austria were curiously two-faced when it came to making a distinction between those marriages which offended their National Socialist sensibilities and those they permitted because it suited them. Not wishing to attract adverse criticism from the international press in the interwar years, the Austrian authorities made a legal distinction between 'privileged' and 'non-privileged' marriages of mixed race. Those in which the husband was of Aryan origin and the primary income earner, or whose children had been baptized, were categorized as 'privileged'. As such, they were permitted to remain in their homes and were entitled to receive the same ration cards as the rest of the population, as well as being exempt from certain laws and taxes. Of more importance, they were safe from deportation.

Oskar Baader and his family were not so fortunate, as his membership of the outlawed Social Democrats deprived them of all privileges afforded to Aryan spouses. This included certain essential foodstuffs denied to Jews, such as meat, wheat, eggs and milk.

Those who had kept their identity and made an effort to establish a relationship with the Jewish community benefited from pooled resources and the sense of unity that gave them a modicum of hope, while those who had turned their back on their roots found themselves belonging to neither one group nor the other and were left to fend for themselves. Children of intermarried families were occasionally welcomed into the Christian community by the Hilfsstelle, a Catholic outreach initiative – provided of course that they had been baptized – although the extent to which they were accepted depended on the willingness of other members to overlook their non-Aryan origins. But even if their friends and neighbours were tolerant, their respective families might not be. Both Jews and non-Jews shunned those who had 'married out' and refused them sanctuary and all other forms of support, making their predicament all the more precarious.

Yellow stars

From 1 September 1941, all Austrian Jews were required by law to wear the distinctive yellow star sewn on to their clothes. This not only made them visible, so they could not risk being seen in public places from which Jews were banned, but vulnerable to abuse and assault. But many of those from mixed marriages risked arrest and deportation by defying the law, so desperate were they to enjoy simple pleasures such as walking in the parks and going to the theatre or cinema.

Life was fraught with danger for both 'privileged' and 'non-privileged' families as they lived with the ever-present threat of being denounced by fanatical National Socialists who sought attention by informing on enemies of the state. Their movements were under almost constant scrutiny, but some found unexpected support from strangers who demonstrated their disapproval of Nazi racist policy by providing food (often anonymously) or in individual acts of kindness that made a difference between life and death.

CZECHOSLOVAKIA – 15 March 1939

A year after Hitler annexed Austria, Nazi Germany swallowed up Czechoslovakia.

It was a pathetic and pitiful sight. The inhabitants of Prague threw snowballs at the columns of German armoured vehicles rolling through the cobbled streets of the Old City because they dared not throw stones. The soldiers didn't know what to make of it. They couldn't fire on the crowd. This was a victory parade celebrating the conquest of a country without a shot having been fired. They were under strict orders to maintain discipline in the ranks and not to retaliate unless they were shot at.

The Nazi newsreel cameras were turning to record the Czechs welcoming the glorious Wehrmacht with the Hitler salute, despite the blizzard that kept so many off the streets. But it wasn't the heavy snow that deterred them. They simply didn't want to believe it. Those who braved the weather stared in stunned silence. Many wept openly and bitterly, for they felt that their country had been sold out by the Allies, who had once sworn to protect it.

Neville Chamberlain, the British prime minister, who was so eager to guarantee 'peace in our time' at any cost, had given in to Hitler at the Munich conference six months earlier. Having been convinced by the dictator's assurance that this would be his 'last territorial demand in

Europe', Chamberlain had conceded to the Reich the predominantly German-speaking Sudetenland in the west of the country. Time would prove the lie, but on this freezing March morning in 1939, it appeared that Czechoslovakia had been sacrificed to ensure the future of Western Europe.

The Czech government of Edvard Beneš had fled to London, leaving the Germans to carve up the country and take over the ministries of defence, foreign affairs, customs and communications. While a token number of Prague's ethnic Germans waved swastika flags for the cameras, the greater number assembled in Wenceslas Square to sing the national anthem, which would be banned the next day when Hitler proclaimed the Nazi Protectorate of Bohemia and Moravia. The Protectorate incorporated the majority Czech-populated areas of what was formerly Czechoslovakia and the majority German-populated Sudetenland. From the remaining territory, the Slovak Republic was created and given token independence as a client state of Nazi Germany. This was headed by a Catholic priest, Jozef Tiso, who became a figurehead for the Slovak population that made up 85 per cent of the state's inhabitants.

Rules and restrictions

The first act of the new Reichsprotektor, Konstantin von Neurath, was to impose a visa system to restrict movement of the citizens and to identify those of Roma and Jewish origin. Many committed suicide rather than live under Nazi rule and risk transportation to concentration camps. Those of non-Roma and Jewish origin were required to produce proof of their 'untainted' ancestry, dating back three generations.

Von Neurath also imposed strict censorship on Czech newspapers, banned democratic opposition parties and disbanded the trade unions.

Every day the newspapers published lists of those executed, imprisoned or transported to concentration camps, so that the population were reminded of what awaited them if they defied Nazi decrees.

Every aspect of public life had to conform to German law. Traffic regulations were introduced, requiring all vehicles to drive on the right-hand side, though few Czechs owned a car. By 1944, all private cars would be banned. Blackouts were imposed to curtail the activities of any opposition groups, as there was no threat from air raids. Following an official boycott of Jewish businesses, shops displayed signs assuring customers that the owners were Aryan.

The Germans then set about indoctrinating the young by banning school textbooks which did not conform to Nazi ideology and introducing those which promoted spurious Nazi racial 'science' and propaganda.

Czech culture was subjected to stringent rules and restrictions with anything that encouraged national pride banned, along with anything the regime considered to conform to their definition of 'decadent' art. Jazz was banned as it was deemed to be 'primitive', 'jungle' music and of no value to white Aryan society. Plays were subject to strict censorship. Cinemas were forbidden from screening all but light comedies and every film had to be accompanied by German subtitles. There were few distractions on offer other than ice hockey and swimming. For ordinary Czechs, the quality of life deteriorated rapidly.

Acts of resistance

The Germans imposed long working hours for those labouring in the armaments factories. It was not uncommon for essential workers to work all day Sunday, for example, to fulfil quotas imposed by their German employers. It has been estimated that Czech factories supplied half the munitions and weapons used in the conquest of Poland, Belgium, Holland and France. Consequently, workers' health declined. Many women chose to become pregnant rather than continue slaving for the Germans, despite the fact that a diet of meagre rations meant they risked malnutrition affecting the health of their child.

Within a month of the German occupation, the mood had darkened considerably and many were expressing the wish that they could throw more than snowballs at the enemy. On 28 October, historically the country's national day of independence, the Nazis banned traditional celebrations. Feelings boiled over and a peaceful demonstration turned violent after 100,000 protestors poured on to the streets in the centre of Prague, pulling down German street signs and chanting anti-German slogans. Memorials to the fallen of the First World War were covered with flowers and statues were draped in the Czech flag that had been banned by the Nazis. The German police responded by opening fire on the crowd, fatally wounding a medical student, Jan Opletal, killing workman Václav Sedláçek and gravely wounding nine others. Four hundred protestors were arrested.

On 15 November, the day Opletal's coffin was carried through the streets to the railway station for burial in his home town; students

A detachment of German troops crosses the river Vltava in Prague, 23 March 1939.

hung black flags from their dormitory windows and staged a second spontaneous demonstration against the occupation, singing the national anthem in defiance of the ban and chanting anti-fascist slogans.

News of Opletal's death and the student protests quickly spread to other Czech cities and more demonstrations were organized in towns across the Protectorate which enraged the Nazis, who could not afford to have their authority publicly challenged by a popular movement that might grow beyond their control.

Two days later, the Germans raided the university, arresting thousands of students and imprisoning them without trial. Nine student leaders were subsequently executed, more than 1,000 were transported to Sachsenhausen concentration camp and the university was closed by order of the Nazi police chief, Karl Hermann Frank.

Hitler's hangman

Frank was continually in conflict with von Neurath, who Hitler felt was too lenient. In September 1941, Himmler's personal aide, Reinhard Heydrich, was sent to the Protectorate to act as von Neurath's deputy.

Heydrich's first act once he had installed himself in Prague's medieval castle was to have the Czech Prime Minister Alois Eliáš arrested and executed for alleged links with the resistance.

Hitler's hangman, as he was known, made it clear that the Czechs had no right to live in the Protectorate. By his definition, 40 per cent of the population were 'mongrels' and 15 per cent 'subhuman', which left 45 per cent to be Germanized.

The ruthless Heydrich was to succeed von Neurath, but on 4 June 1942, after just eight months in office, Heydrich was assassinated by members of the Czech underground, an act which remains one of the most significant acts of resistance against the Nazi occupation of Europe.

It is believed to have been the brainchild of exiled president, Edvard Beneš, who desperately wanted to remind the world that his country had been betrayed by the political appeasers, but that it would not simply submit quietly to Nazi tyranny without a fight.

Tragically, the Czechs paid a terrible price for their symbolic act of defiance. More than 1,300 civilians were murdered and the villages of Lidice and Ležáky were burned to the ground, though the assassins had no connection with either village. Pregnant women were subjected to forced abortions in the hospital where Heydrich had died and children were taken from their parents and sent to Germany, where their identities and past were erased and they were to be brought up as Aryans.

Hitler afforded his protégé a Nazi state funeral, though in private he condemned Heydrich as 'stupid and idiotic' for having exposed himself to danger by riding in an open top car and keeping to a predictable routine, which just invited an assassination attempt.

The Three Kings

With fear of German reprisals, the Czech underground concentrated on waging a war of information, supplying the Allies with details of German troop movements, ammunition trains and other vital strategic help.

The Germans were desperate to stop this information reaching London and set out to capture the leaders of the main Czech resistance group they code-named the Three Kings.

Josef Balabán, Josef Mašín and Václav Morávek were all former Czech army officers who knew that gathering the right sort of information could be just as damaging to the enemy as a well-placed bomb if the Allies acted on it, but they also published anti-Nazi pamphlets and helped smuggle Special Operations Executive (SOE) agents and Allied pilots to safety so that they could continue the fight.

Their main sources were members of the Czech police who worked as translators as well as railway workers and postal workers who intercepted mail.

Unlike other resistance groups in occupied Europe, the three men took their fight to the heart of the Nazi state with bomb attacks in Munich, Leipzig and Berlin. Mašín's brother-in-law, Ctirad Novák, was working as a double agent and as such had access to ministries and Nazi offices. In January 1941, he placed suitcase bombs in the Berlin Police Headquarters and the Ministry of Air Travel, both of which did considerable damage and perhaps, more importantly, they demonstrated that the resistance could reach into the lair of the beast itself.

Their most audacious act was an attempt to assassinate SS Reichsführer Heinrich Himmler. The bomb went off as scheduled, but Himmler escaped injury as his train was delayed.

The group also derailed several troop transports by disguising bombs as coal – when the fake fuel was thrown in the boiler, the engines exploded.

Tragically, in April 1941 in Prague, Balabán was arrested, tortured and executed.

Mašín's speciality was supplying the resistance with weapons which he took from the Ruzyně barracks. He drove in disguised as a Nazi soldier, loaded his car with guns and ammunition and drove out unchallenged. In June 1942, he too was arrested, tortured and executed without revealing the identities of his associates.

Morávek was a devout Christian who always carried a pocket Bible and two pistols. He proudly proclaimed that he believed in both God and guns and it was his faith in both that prompted him to carry out some of his most audacious and dangerous activities. Though a wanted man, he would deliver copies of the underground magazine *V Boj* to Gestapo headquarters and once walked into a bar frequented by Oskar Fleischer, the Gestapo agent who had been assigned to hunt him down. He even offered to light Fleischer's cigarette and walked out alive without being recognized. Later, he sent Fleischer's superior in the Gestapo a letter boasting of the incident, in the hope of discrediting Fleischer and claimed that his actions had been a bet which left him 1,000 crowns the richer.

Sadly, Morávek's luck ran out in March 1942, when he was shot during a gun battle with the Gestapo.

The sacrifice of Czechoslovakia

After the massacre of Lidice and Ležáky, the Czechs had little appetite for armed resistance, fearing that whatever damage they could inflict on the hated enemy would not be justified by the reprisals meted out to their fellow citizens.

It was therefore not until the autumn of 1944, when the end of the Third Reich seemed to be in sight, that the Czech resistance made its presence felt in both the Slovak Republic and the Protectorate. In the Slovak Republic, the primary target was the country's pro-Nazi paramilitary organization, the Hlinka Guard. Supported by the Germans who were not ready to retreat, the Guard inflicted heavy losses on the

Slovaks, many of whom escaped into the mountains and waited for the Soviets to drive the Germans out of their country.

This left the unarmed civilians defenceless against Hitler's vindictive rage. But they were determined to avenge themselves on their oppressors even if they stood little chance of winning. When it was rumoured that Hitler had ordered the destruction of Prague in the last months of the war, people spilled out on the streets of the capital tearing down German signs, erecting barricades and storming the radio station. The Germans attacked, but were driven back. Fighting continued as rumours of the Russian advance emboldened the inhabitants to take back their city before the Soviets arrived. The Americans under General George S. Patton had been ordered to halt at Pilsen, to allow the Russians to take the city.

Even after Hitler's suicide on 30 April 1945 and the surrender of German forces in Europe on 7 May, the Germans continued fighting and destroying historic buildings that had no strategic importance until the Russians arrived on 9 May, bringing the occupation of Czechoslovakia to an end. Two thousand Czechs died in the last days of fighting to liberate their city, only for the Red Army to march in and subject them to four decades of communist dictatorship. But Czech historian Jaroslav Hrbek believes that their sacrifice was necessary:

> It was just the thing the morale of the nation needed, just to show to themselves that they were able to resist, that they were able to fight actively against the Germans. In that sense I would say that those two thousand dead in Prague made the sacrifice for the right cause and helped *to restore the morality and the self-assurance of the nation.*

Holiday in the Protectorate – reality TV's take on the occupation

It is impossible to imagine how difficult life was like for the civilian population in the occupied countries. Even those who lived through those times are prone to selective impressions and fading memories. The only way to convey how harsh life was during the war years is to recreate it – at least, that is exactly what a Czech television show has done.

Holiday in the Protectorate is unquestionably one of the most bizarre and controversial reality television shows ever conceived and is one which has divided Czechs into those who find it entertaining and educational, and those who consider its sanitized, soap operatic approach in extremely bad taste.

The eight episodes broadcast in 2015 by public broadcaster CT TV put three generations of one family in period costume and provided them with the rations and other restrictions endured by their grandparents during those five and a half years of Nazi rule. They were housed in a typical cottage in the Czech countryside and had to remain isolated from the outside world for two months. To recreate the oppressive atmosphere of the era, actors were cast as Nazis and Gestapo informers and were instructed to behave toward the family as their historical counterparts might have done. German soldiers woke them in the middle of the night, rummaged through their belongings and interrogated them, though no one was actually tortured, as their real-life counterparts would have been.

The actors were instructed to improvise to keep the situation moving and the project was supervised by two historians to ensure it remained faithful and accurate. One of them denied that it trivialized the trauma that Czechs went through, while the producer claimed its primary aim was to encourage viewers to ask what they would have done in that situation.

Historian Stanislav Kokoska was not entirely convinced: 'They know what the result of the war was. They know they will not be killed. So they can play a part and cast themselves as the hero.'

His criticism is borne out in episodes where the family defy the Gestapo and are allowed to walk away, something that would not have happened in real life.

Each week the cast were faced with a new challenge. These were both practical and moral challenges, ranging from milking a cow and coping with primitive outdoor plumbing to being asked to hide a resistance fighter or obtain provisions on the black market.

Viewing figures were only modest and the critics were divided, but it did appear to have raised awareness of the grim realities of that era among teenagers.

CHAPTER 2
A RACIAL WAR

POLAND – 1 September 1939

Few countries suffered as much under Nazi occupation as Poland. The country became a symbol of Hitler's vindictive rage and an example of the punishment he would mete out to those who defied him. The destruction of Warsaw in September 1940, which left half of the capital in ruins and an estimated 60,000 civilians dead, was a warning to other nations of what would become of them if they resisted the Führer's demands. Nazi Germany would make no distinction between civilians and combatants.

Typically, the Nazis attempted to blame others for their own crimes. After the invasion, with the city in a state of devastation, posters were put up that showed a disdainful Chamberlain turning away from a grieving Pole with the caption, 'England, This Is Your Doing!'

Soon the posters would name those who had been arrested and executed on the dubious pretext of having committed crimes such as sabotage or possession of weapons, though the condemned had frequently done little more than deface German propaganda posters or fail to show respect for a German officer they had passed in the street. The death penalty was handed down to Poles with casual abandon.

Warsaw was not the worst hit, however. In western Poland, 50,000 civilians were murdered in reprisals for alleged 'atrocities', such as the incident on 1 September 1939, two days after the invasion, when it was said that an angry mob of Poles killed tens of thousands of their civilian, ethnic German neighbours. At least, that was the claim made by Nazi propaganda. In fact, no more than 100 German insurgents had been killed in what was a firefight with a retreating Polish artillery unit in the town of Bydgoszcz (Bromberg). The punishment dealt to those suspected of belonging to this army of shadows was hugely disproportionate to the number of alleged victims. Mobile SS killing squads and vigilante groups roamed the region slaughtering Poles, Jews and Gentiles alike and driving terrified Poles toward the capital.

Such retaliation for imaginary atrocities committed by Poles on ethnic Germans was a mere pretext under which could be carried out the true purpose of the Nazis' invasion: wholesale ethnic cleansing. As he had admitted to his High Command prior to the invasion, Hitler was determined to 'destroy Poland' – it was this that motivated him, not the acquisition of territory or the plundering of resources.

Poland divided

Western Poland was assimilated into the Reich, while eastern Poland was annexed by the Soviets. The remainder, a portion encompassing Warsaw, Krakow and Lublin, housed the 'General Government'. This was mainly staffed by low-ranking Polish civil servants and local mayors, except in Galicia, where the Ukrainians administered German laws under the watchful eye of Governor-General Hans Frank, the self-styled 'King of Poland'.

It was Frank who, like some ogre in a Grimm fairy tale, organized the abduction of 'Aryan'-looking children from Poland and their adoption in Germany by committed Nazi foster parents, who took an oath never to reveal the true identity of the children or their origins.

Their biological parents would either perish in the mass executions, starve in a country stripped of resources or be transported to Germany to serve as slave labourers with a 'P' stitched into their ragged clothes to indicate their origin.

Poles immediately became second-class citizens in their own country, banned from city centres and restricted to travelling in the back of trams while their conquerors reserved the more comfortable front section for themselves. Germans were prohibited from socializing with Poles to the extent that many cafés were designated 'Poles only' and Germans were ordered not to share a table with any Pole in other eating places. Casinos, cinemas and municipal buildings were commandeered by the Germans, who hung the swastika from their balconies to announce their presence.

Formerly Hitler's legal adviser, Hans Frank (left) was appointed governor-general of the occupied Polish territories and conducted a reign of terror against the civilian population, including extermination and enslavement.

Divide and conquer

The Germans adopted a 'divide and conquer' policy in Poland as they would do elsewhere in Europe, drafting the country's civil servants, mayors and other officials to administer their laws and do much of their dirty work for them. In this way, they did not have to allocate men and resources to do mundane administrative duties and at the same time they could delegate responsibility to the local leaders, provided these people were supervised by a suitable zealous National Socialist. In Warsaw, this meant that the city's 30,000 civil servants were all Poles familiar with the language and the region. German instructions would be carried out by the 16,000-strong Polish Blue Police, whom Frank tasked with sending 'their fellow countrymen to their doom'.

Tragically for the Jews, the Polish resistance had no interest in intervening on their behalf. As Peter Fritzsche notes in his book *An Iron Wind: Europe Under Hitler*, 'because the violence of the German invasion precluded collaboration, the anti-German front was extremely broad politically and included extreme Polish nationalists and anti-Semites.' In the other occupied countries, anti-Semites collaborated with the Nazis; in Poland, anti-Semites were imprisoned by the Nazis. The Polish inmates of Auschwitz included many fascists as Polish patriotism and anti-Semitism were not seen as mutually exclusive.

The Mouth of the Tiger

'I stand in a cage before a hungry and angry tiger. I stuff his mouth with meat, the flesh of my brothers and sisters, to keep him in his cage lest he breaks loose and tears us all to bits.'
Moses Merin, member of the Jewish Council, Sosnowiec 1943

When the Jews of the Warsaw ghetto rose up against the Germans in April 1943, they did so without the help of the Polish underground, which stood by and watched them fight a heroic but ultimately futile battle of attrition. The plight of the Jews received scant mention in the underground press in occupied countries and was most conspicuously absent from the underground press in Poland. Even where it did receive attention, for example in the Home Army's weekly *Biuletyn Informacyjny*, the suffering of the Jews was pitched alongside that of the Poles. The circular spoke of the Jews as being 'systematically slain in our country', making a distinction between the way Jews and Poles were treated. *Biuletyn Informacyjny* saw the occupation in terms of Catholic martyrdom, the latest in a long line of suffering imposed by foreign invaders.

By turning their backs on the Jews, the Poles imagined that they might survive simply because they were not Jews; they were not the primary target for the Germans. It is revealing that a Home Army leaflet issued in the summer of 1943 condemned the murder of 1,000 Poles by the Nazis as 'the largest mass murder in the capital', while ignoring the killing of 300,000 Jews during the destruction of the Warsaw ghetto.

The Jew hunt

'The world is viewing this crime, more horrible than anything else in the annals of mankind, and is silent. The slaughter of millions of defenceless people is taking place amid ominous general silence... That silence can no longer be tolerated... Whoever remains silent in the face of murder becomes the murderer's accomplice. Who does not condemn it, condones it.'

Zofia Kossak-Szczucka, August 1942

Dr Zygmunt Klukowski in Szczebrzeszyn recorded in his diary in 1942, 'People walking on the street are so used to seeing corpses on the sidewalks that they pass by without any emotion.' As many of these bodies were those of starved Poles, it was not surprising that the fate of the Jews elicited even less interest from their Catholic neighbours.

'It's hard to believe but the attitude towards Jews is changing,' he added. 'There are many people who see the Jews not as human beings, but as animals that must be destroyed.'

And yet there were thought to be up to 90,000 Poles who risked their lives and that of their friends and families to give shelter to 28,000 Jews in the months before the Warsaw uprising.

In the two big round-ups of August and October 1942, Dr Klukowski observed Poles joining the 'Jew hunt', rifling through their abandoned belongings that had been collected by municipal workers and stealing the choicest items. The orderly elimination of the Jews and their apparent passivity – despite this being contradicted by the number of battered bodies left behind – gave rise to the myth that the Jews had meekly acceded to their deaths, which only fuelled the contempt felt by the Poles towards their Jewish compatriots.

Even the Catholic writer and resistance fighter Zofia Kossak-Szczucka, who assisted hundreds of Jews with fleeing Nazi persecution and who damned those who stood by and watched their persecution as being complicit in those atrocities, held that the Jews were 'political, ideological and economic enemies of Poland'.

An anonymous adviser to the Polish government in exile declared, 'If the mass of the Jews ever return, our population will not recognize their restitution claims, but will treat them instead as invaders, resisting them by violent means if need be.'

But there was no need to fear their return. The majority were already long dead by the time Poland was under Soviet control.

Inevitably, after the last Jews had been transported, the Germans came for the Poles, deporting young men to forced labour camps and factories in Germany. In a process that contrasted starkly with the round-up of the Jews, who had been escorted through the streets by a few policemen wielding batons, the young Poles were marched to the railway marshalling yards under armed guard. Rumours then began circulating that the Germans were coming for the elderly, who would be murdered in their own homes in the next stage, the intention being to eliminate all witnesses to the German atrocities.

The Polish economist Kazimierz Wyka summed up the situation with typical Polish irony:

> Shielded by the sword of the German executioner, who was carrying out a crime never before seen in history, the Polish shopkeeper took possession of the keys to the till of his Jewish competitor and believed that he was acting in the most moral manner. To the Germans are left the guilt and the crime, to us the keys and the till.

But the Germans didn't have it all their own way. Polish railways workers could not be supervised as easily as the clerks and bureaucrats. They disrupted transport and stole coal and tools to sell on the black market.

A question of purity

Not all Poles were resigned to 'internal exile' or passive resistance. Many Poles took advantage of the opportunity to prove their Aryan ancestry and became officially German. It was a gruelling process, but many were prepared to jump through hoops and provide proof of their 'racial purity' in order to preserve their property and jobs, and to secure larger rations and other privileges, even if it meant severing all contact with former friends and neighbours.

The rest lived on their nerves. Any moment could bring the screech of brakes below in the street, the rush of footsteps on the stairs, the knock at the door. Sleep was fitful and filled with nightmares, daytime brought a constant anxious wait for news and search for food. And the reward for standing in line for hours might be a loaf of badly baked bread that smelt old, felt soft and tasted like 'one part soaked newspaper and one part old dust rag'.

The Poles lived one day at a time, sometimes hour by hour. Each day they survived was a small victory, with a restless sleep as their reward.

Many sought a brief respite from the relentless dreariness in drink. Cafés and bars were opened in every vacant lot where boarded-up shops and houses had been. Within two years of the occupation, there were more than 500 bars and cafés in the capital, all turning a profitable business, the only profitable and growing business in Poland outside the black market.

The underground press condemned the increase in alcoholism and petty crime, but their appeals fell on deaf ears. They threatened to publish the names of young women who were seen fraternizing with German soldiers and they issued 'ten commandments for the civil struggle' which instructed all Poles to avoid 'cultural, social and business relations' with the occupation forces.

The Allies had declared war on Germany in September 1939, after delivering an ultimatum to Hitler to withdraw his forces from Poland. But when he refused to do so, they failed to come to Poland's aid. The country was left to endure five years of Nazi barbarity on a scale the world could scarcely imagine.

A racial war

'In Prague, big red posters were put up on which one could read that seven Czechs had been shot today. I said to myself, "If I had to put up a poster for every seven Poles shot, the forests of Poland would not be sufficient to manufacture the paper."'

Hans Frank, Governor-General of Poland,
in *Völkischer Beobachter*, 6 June 1940

Life was cheap in Poland during the occupation. The Germans considered the Poles to be an inferior race to be denigrated and despised, while Polish

Jews, Romanies and Slavs were *Untermenschen*, subhuman and likened to 'vermin', to be worked to death or exterminated if they were too old or sick to serve the Master Race.

The new masters had no interest in keeping the population above basic subsistence level. Anything beyond that was a waste of food as far as they were concerned and would be better shipped back to the Reich to feed the mothers and children of the Fatherland.

As a result of their systematic murder, enslavement and starvation of 'undesirables', the Germans reduced the population of Poland by a fifth, only half of the victims being Jews.

The occupation of countries in Northern and Western Europe was said to be driven by the need for *Lebensraum*, living space for *Volksdeutsche*, the ethnic Germans assimilated into the Reich by the seizure of territories that Hitler believed had been unlawfully taken by the Allies at the end of the First World War. In repossessing these countries, the Nazi state would acquire their natural resources and industry.

But the invasion of Poland and the Slavic countries in Eastern Europe was undertaken only partly to strip the East of its industry and the resources necessary to sustain the German war machine. The primary reason was to eradicate the 'inferior' races and, in doing so, render the country safe for Aryan settlement. In this respect, the invasion of Poland and the ethnic cleansing or genocide was part of a racial war.

The death squads

> 'A thousand years will pass and still this guilt of Germany will not have been erased.'
>
> Hans Frank during his trial at Nuremberg

In the wake of the German advance, two million Poles were forcibly evicted from their homes and driven out of western Poland to make way for the German settlers. They were transported by train or marched under guard to a region designated as the General Government, a Nazi slave state ruled by Hans Frank. Frank was instructed to destroy the economic, cultural and political structure and leave 'nothing but rubble'.

The former lawyer was given the power of life and death over 35 million people and just days after the defeat of Poland, on 3 October 1939, he addressed German army officers and informed them that he intended to 'remove all supplies, raw materials, machines, factories, installations, etc. which are important for the German war economy', leaving only what was necessary for 'bare existence'.

Polish factories were gutted, their equipment shipped to Germany or handed to German businessmen and officials to be run with ruthless efficiency.

And to demonstrate their ruthlessness, Poland's political and religious leaders and intellectual elite were rounded up and executed – 60,000 people in all – to leave the general population leaderless and in no doubt as to what would happen to anyone who opposed the New Order.

The systematic murders of thousands of doctors, academics, lawyers, Catholic priests and members of the Polish aristocracy were carried out by the *Einsatzgruppen*, execution squads. Tens of thousands more were shipped to concentration camps.

An underground education

Schools were closed; any allowed to remain open were primary school level and restricted to teaching basic skills, so that the next generation of Poles could do little more than count to 500 and write their own name. But the Poles refused to roll over and play dead. They set up underground schools and even a university which issued certificates to its 2,500 students. However, this crime saw an estimated 8,500 teachers later arrested and the majority executed.

Many students were actively involved in the resistance, both in the Home Army and in the printing and distribution of forged documents, ration cards and newspapers, of which there were said to be 1,000, with 300 published periodically during the occupation. The Home Army were armed and equipped by the British and so were able to engage the Germans in a number of large-scale battles, although they were mainly deployed in small hit-and-run skirmishes to sow fear and uncertainty among the occupation forces.

Collective responsibility

In violation of the rules of war and of the Hague Convention, the Nazis introduced the policy of collective responsibility, under which any acts of sabotage or armed resistance were to be punished by the imprisonment and execution of friends, family members and neighbours of those suspected of carrying out the acts. For every German affected, be they soldier or civilian, the Germans rounded up 100 Poles at random and held them as hostages until those responsible surrendered, to be executed without trial. Often the hostages were killed regardless of whether those responsible turned themselves in or not.

Hostages were also taken from lists of prominent citizens compiled by the Gestapo, so that the population were deprived of leaders, doctors, teachers, lawyers and others who were vital to the life of the community.

However, the Nazis were not satisfied with terrorizing the Poles, they wanted to humiliate them and crush their spirit, so they hanged many of the saboteurs and anyone who defied them from lamp-posts as a warning to others.

News of the atrocities soon reached the Allies, prompting British Prime Minister Winston Churchill to condemn the Nazis:

> Every week (Hitler's) firing parties are busy in a dozen lands. Mondays he shoots Dutchmen, Tuesdays, Norwegians, Wednesdays, French or Belgians stand against the wall. Thursdays it is the Czechs who must suffer and now there are the Serbs and the Greeks to fill his repulsive bill of executions. But always, all the days, there are the Poles.

Censorship and publication

The conquerors instigated a policy of food rationing to starve the Poles into submission that went further than the rationing they had imposed on other Europeans. It was forbidden for Polish farmers to supply agricultural produce to the cities, which led to a thriving black market and prohibitively expensive prices for staple foods such as potatoes and meat, while bread had to be baked from sawdust-mixed flour to give it substance.

Every effort was made to eradicate Polish culture by burning books and banning the performance of Polish music and plays, but the underground ensured these survived by organizing clandestine concerts and performances on temporary stages in private apartments, cellars and attics.

The Polish national anthem was banned and anyone heard singing or even humming it could be summarily executed. Polish monuments were smashed and street names renamed in German.

The underground press also printed academic textbooks in the belief that, though the body might be enslaved and starved, the mind should be free and nourished, especially if Poland was to survive the occupation. But the Germans were printing too; 32 million propaganda leaflets were produced, warning of the imminent threat to the country posed by the Russians. They appealed to Polish patriots by citing the Polish–Soviet war of 1920 and the decisive Battle of Warsaw, which had seen the Russians defeated. But few were persuaded to take up arms and fight alongside the invader when they saw how the Germans were mistreating their people, who were forced to live on fewer than 700 calories a day, about a third of the healthy requirement for an adult.

Vast numbers of Poles suffered physically and succumbed to disease through malnutrition. In the last year of the war, six per cent of the population, that is to say one and a half million people, had contracted tuberculosis.

Tragically, those who managed to survive privation, disease and persecution were likely to be suspected of having been a collaborator and were consequently shot by the Soviets when they overran the country in January 1945. The Home Army were also known to kill Jews after they returned to their homes, having risked their lives fighting the Germans for the previous five years.

Concentration camps

'It is essential that the great German people should consider it as its major task to destroy all Poles.'

Adolf Hitler

The degree of persecution suffered by the Poles is evidenced by the 2,000 concentration camps the Germans built in the country. Although Polish Jews were numerically the largest group of victims of Nazi genocide, hundreds of thousands of Polish Christians were murdered or died from maltreatment at the hands of the occupation forces. In addition to the three million Polish Jews who were killed, half of Poland's academics, lawyers and journalists were killed and an estimated three million ethnic Poles perished as a result of Nazi policy.

But the German pathological obsession with detail and bureaucracy saw some of their intended prey slip through their fingers. Piotr Szafranski cites the example of his grandfather, an Austrian by birth who was working in Poland as a schoolteacher. After receiving an official summons from the occupation authorities to pack a suitcase and report for deportation, he dutifully did as he was ordered, even though he could have appealed as he had served in the Austrian army in 1914. But when the truck came to take him to the railway station, there was confusion over his identity as his name had been misspelled. And although Szafranski argued that he was indeed the man they were supposed to take, the Germans refused and instead took another man with a similar-sounding name so that they could fulfil their quota.

Their destination was Auschwitz and the man who took Szafranski's place was dead within six months. His family were offered his ashes if they would pay for the urn and shipping.

A tourist's guide to Nazi-occupied Poland

In the years before the Second World War, every serious tourist travelled with their Baedeker guide close at hand. The little red book was as essential as their passport. It was up to date, reliable and accurate, so much so that during the war, Luftwaffe chief Hermann Göring was said to refer to a copy of *Baedeker's Great Britain* when planning air raids on London and other major cities. The raids became known as the 'Baedeker raids' because they appeared to target buildings of cultural rather than military significance.

But even Baedeker was not immune to National Socialist propaganda as its 1943 guide to occupied Poland, *Baedeker's Generalgouvernement*, revealed.

The war had cut the German publisher off from their traditional customers, so they turned instead to publishing guides for the German 'visitor' to occupied Europe. The intended readership included the Wehrmacht, German businessmen and the regime's civilian administrators, as well as those ethnic Germans who had been 'resettled' in regions formerly occupied by Jews and other indigenous groups who had been forcibly evicted or murdered.

Naturally, no mention of these former inhabitants or their culture was to be found in the hitherto reliable and comprehensive guides whose publication was now partly funded by the state. The publisher had suffered declining sales in the early 1930s until the National Socialists bailed them out with a massive loan in October 1934. At that time, the new guides were to be published only in German (previously they had been available in German, French and English) and were to concentrate on holiday destinations covered by the *Kraft durch Freude* ('Strength

Through Joy') state-sponsored leisure organization. Tourism was deemed to be 'a matter of state concern' and consequently brought under state censorship and supervision.

Poland for the German 'visitor'

The Nazis were fixated on how Germany was perceived by the rest of the world, an obsession which reached a peak with the publication of its 1936 guide to Germany, which was timed to coincide with the summer Olympics held in Berlin. Anyone reading between the lines would have noticed the telling discrepancy in the population statistics which only showed figures for Germans of Protestant and Catholic origin, a total which did not add up to 100 per cent. A section on recent history also referred to the Nuremberg Laws of 1935 as pertaining to issues of citizenship, rather than racist laws excluding Jews from public life.

It was therefore not surprising that Baedeker's guide to occupied Poland painted a highly selective and rosy picture of life under Nazi tyranny. The *Generalgouvernement* covered only central and southern Poland and part of Galicia, which were collectively designated a 'dependency' of the Reich.

Its content suggests it was largely compiled by clerks and officials working for the Nazi Governor-General Hans Frank, whose primary purpose was to justify the occupation on the lines that the region was historically German. As the preface notes, the guide will identify 'the innumerable vestiges, often hidden, of old German cultural and pioneering activities – above all, the creations of German architecture.'

The visitor is informed that the language may sound difficult at first, but that a fifth of all Polish words are of German origin. Besides, owners of the better class hotels are now German, as are all railway officials and other administration staff, with the exception of small rural stations. Those uncomfortable about the prospect of sharing a railway carriage or a waiting room with Poles are reassured that facilities exclusively for the use of German nationals are provided. Travel by road is discouraged, particularly at night, though no reason is given other than the poor state of the roads.

But in other respects, the German 'visitor' will be well rewarded, as no ration cards are required for cheese and eggs, while the meat ration is twice what it is in Germany.

There is no lack of entertainment with cinemas screening only German language films, theatres offering German comedy and drama, and numerous bars, nightclubs and cafés patronized by German soldiers, making it safe for the tourist to enjoy the nightlife. But the emphasis is on culture, German culture that has been erroneously attributed to Polish artists.

In a chapter on the arts by Professor Frey of Breslau University, all major works of art to be found in Poland are of German origin. Under this spurious pretext, many of Poland's art treasures were shipped back to the Reich, some of them designated for Hitler's proposed *Führermuseum* to be built in Linz, the rest appropriated by Göring and other Nazi 'art collectors'. No wonder almost all of Poland's museums were closed during the war – they were probably empty.

A *Judenfrei* map

Although tourists with a liking for culture were more likely to visit churches than synagogues, Baedeker's rival guides identified Poland's Jewish quarters and places of worship as being worth a visit. The Nazi-era Baedeker, however, avoids any mention of Poland's Jewish heritage and makes one telling remark in referring to the Jews in the past tense, while noting that Krakow and Lublin are now '*Judenfrei*' – free of Jews. Many of Poland's synagogues had been demolished by the Nazis, but they are not even referred to as having existed or having been of historical or architectural interest, though rival guides single out Warsaw's main synagogue for its cupola designed by Leandro Marconi. Baedeker omits all mention of the sizeable Jewish population of Warsaw, as if they had never existed, while its highly detailed maps exclude all sites of Jewish interest. Historic Jewish cemeteries, such as those in Warsaw and Lvov, are a blank space in Baedeker. In a passing reference to the conspicuous absence of millions of Polish Jews, Baedeker merely states that they had been 'moved out', though the word used ('*aussiedeln*') translates more accurately as 'evacuated', with the connotation of this being in a hurry and a disorganized, brusque manner. As Nicholas Lane observes in his essay, 'Tourism in Nazi-Occupied Poland: Baedeker's *Generalgouvernement*', the book 'is a propaganda text rather well disguised as a guidebook'.

NORWAY – 9 April 1940

When Norway was invaded on 9 April 1940, military resistance crumbled in eight weeks, but the population were evidently not ready to concede defeat. With little chance of inflicting serious damage on the Wehrmacht and few friends inside the puppet administration, it was left to individuals and organizations to make their displeasure known and to attempt to sabotage or at least slow the machinery of tyranny.

The first sign of national solidarity came with the wearing of the seemingly innocuous paperclip, which symbolized unity. Its origins are unknown, but word soon spread that it signified defiance without the risk of reprisals. The Germans simply didn't notice it and those who did could have had no idea of its significance.

But the novelty soon wore off and there was a need to show open allegiance to their exiled monarch, King Haakon VII, who had publicly defied German demands to appoint Norwegian fascist Vidkun Quisling as Hitler's representative in Norway.

The Norwegians began to wear the royal monogram sewn into their lapels and to sport a flower on the king's birthday. This enraged the Germans, who ordered that the lapels and flowers be torn off, which only emboldened the wearers to sew razors and sharp-edged knife blades behind the emblems to deter the fascist thugs.

When Quisling assumed the role of nominal head of the Nazi government, a campaign of passive resistance gathered momentum, with various groups taking a stand against specific Nazi policies rubber-stamped by the traitor's regime. Quisling's creation of a fascist youth organization modelled on the Hitler Youth provoked the mass resignation of the country's bishops, while his interference in the education system led to a mass strike by the nation's teachers. It was the single most significant act of defiance against the occupation.

School's out

The strike began when Quisling issued a proclamation on 5 February 1942 requiring all teachers to join a new organization under fascist control, the Quisling Teachers' Union, or Laerersamband. But he had underestimated the resentment felt by the vast majority of Norwegians, who saw his assumption of the role of head of state as taking a position that rightly belonged to the king.

The resistance mobilized the teachers to produce a statement in which they declared their refusal to be coerced into joining a political association. It is estimated that as many as 10,000 of the country's 12,000 teachers signed. There was a feeling that strength in numbers would protect individual members from persecution. Initially, this proved to be the case.

Running battles took place between German and Norwegian forces in the Ofotfjord leading to Narvik, Norway in the spring of 1940.

There was nothing the authorities could do but close the schools and sweat it out. The strike lasted a month, though many teachers continued to teach their pupils privately. Unfortunately, while 100,000 parents expressed their support for the strike, twice as many wrote to the regime demanding that they settle the strike as soon as possible so they could get back to work.

The Nazis wouldn't be defied and ordered the government to crack down, with the result that 1,000 teachers – all of them men – were imprisoned. They had hoped that their sheer number would deter the Germans from rounding them up, but Quisling and his Nazi masters could not afford to lose face even if it meant filling the already overcrowded prisons.

The resistance eased the financial burden on the teachers' families by making small payments to compensate for the loss of income, but they couldn't allay the fear they felt for their menfolk, who were at the mercy of the Gestapo.

After almost two months, the teachers refused to return to work or to join the new union, prompting the administration to send half of the hostages to a concentration camp at Kirkenes, where they were forced to work in inhumane conditions. They maintained their morale by organizing classes in which they would teach the others their chosen subject and share their knowledge and they were heartened to learn that the population was behind them. Farmers and students had lined the route that brought them to the camp and offered them food. But once they were behind the barbed wire, they had no news of the situation in the rest of the country.

Then in May, after a month in the camp, they received word that the administration had relented. They would no longer be required to join the fascist union, though they were prevented from returning to work until November, when Quisling finally accepted the fact that passive resistance had worn him down and that he had lost the authority he had hoped to wield over his own countrymen.

Special Unit Lola

Quisling was the most prominent of the traitors, so much so that his name became synonymous with collaborators, but there were many Norwegian fascists who willingly co-operated with the occupation because they believed in the Nazi Aryan myth. None were more despised

Vidkun Quisling (right) gives the Nazi salute. Quisling founded the Norwegian fascist party Nasjonal Samling (National Union) and headed up the pro-Nazi puppet government of Norway during the war. He was executed for high treason in 1945.

by their own people than those who volunteered to join Sonderabteilung Lola (Special Unit Lola), a group of between 60 and 70 men and women who were trained to infiltrate the resistance.

They cynically exploited the fact that most Norwegians believed that their neighbours shared their hatred of the Nazis and so engaged them in casual conversation in public places and on buses and trains hoping they might incriminate themselves. Those suspected of being actively involved in the underground were arrested and tortured in the hope that they might inform on their friends. Others were tricked into believing that they were assisting the resistance by helping their new 'friends' when in fact, they were unwittingly helping the Gestapo.

It is thought that the group were responsible for the arrest and torture of several hundred members of the Norwegian underground – possibly as many as a thousand – and the deaths of at least 80 individuals.

Forty-one members of the group were put on trial after the war and convicted of treason. Ten of the men were executed by firing squad. The remainder received long prison sentences. Their leader Henry Rinnan was personally responsible for the torture and murder of many of their victims and was sentenced to death after the war. In 1944, he had received the Iron Cross Second Class for his services to the Reich.

The New Order in Europe

'Europe united under German leadership in the struggle against Bolshevism and plutocratic powers, alien to Europe'.

Nazi slogan

Though it seems extraordinary now, the Nazi leadership believed that after the war was won, the conquered nations would cease to consider themselves as being occupied and instead see themselves as citizens of a unified, Aryanized Europe.

For that reason, neither Hitler nor his ministers made public pronouncements regarding the future of Europe during the war for fear of making enemies 'prematurely and unnecessarily'. The Führer was acutely aware that extreme nationalist parties in each country would expect to be granted autonomy over their own people as a reward for collaborating with the Reich, but that they would not necessarily be inclined to co-operate with Germany merely because they shared a racist, fascist or extremist ideology.

Even within the Nazi hierarchy, the various personalities and self-interest groups could not agree on how they envisaged governing the New Order and what they wanted from it. Hitler and Himmler were at odds as to how many people would come under control of the regime once the 'inferior' races had been exterminated or deported to slave labour camps. Hitler talked of a core population of up to 90 million Germans, whereas the SS Reichsführer spoke of as many as 120 million 'Germanic' people living and working for the state in the *Grossraumwirtschaft*, or 'greater economic area' of Central and Eastern Europe.

As Philip Morgan, lecturer in contemporary European history and author of *Hitler's Collaborators* observes, 'The idea of interlocking complementary national economies [...] was to achieve [...] self-sufficiency of the continent as a whole.' There would be a division of labour with each country producing what it produced best, in order that it utilized its labour force and resources to its greatest advantage and could then compete globally, though the dictatorship did not take into account the possibility that many democratic countries would not wish to do business with the Nazi state.

IOU

In August 1942, Göring convened a summit of civil and military leaders from each of the occupied countries of Northern and Western Europe in Berlin. They were asked to provide solutions to the increasing food shortage in both Germany and the conquered territories, but it quickly deteriorated into a bragging match, with the 'Fat Man' calling for unfeasible production quotas that he was conjuring out of the air and his audience responding enthusiastically by promising to exceed those targets. As Professor Morgan notes, 'This was a characteristic Nazi procedure, which served to galvanize Nazi leaders into action by setting competitive and impossible targets, in the full expectation that they would be met in a supreme and ruthless act of will.'

However, the entire Nazi economic system was as flawed and corrupt as the personalities who created and controlled it. As Professor Morgan explains, the way in which the Nazis traded with the occupied countries meant that the Reich became a 'permanent creditor', purchasing goods and raw materials in what amounted to a 'limitless IOU scam'.

The National Socialist Norwegian finance minister summed up the win-win situation for the occupation forces when he told Quisling, 'If

Germany loses the war, she will not be able to pay, and if she wins the war, it is questionable whether she will want to pay.'

The Norwegians appear to have been the only occupied country to have benefitted economically and materially from the enforced presence of a foreign military power. Germany had to import significant quantities of food to feed the population whose skilled workforce was needed to operate its factories to capacity. In addition, if Norway's hydroelectric power plants and its aluminium industry were to fulfil their wartime targets, a considerable investment had to be made beyond that which the country would have made in peacetime to provide its domestic needs.

But elsewhere, the primary aim of the Nazi leadership was the plunder and exploitation of each country's economic and natural resources.

Business profited from its compulsory association with the National Socialist state thanks in part to the abolition of trade unions and the regime's ruthless disregard for competitive fair play. But if the collaborators imagined that they would enjoy any serious form of partnership with a totalitarian regime after the war was won, they would have been bitterly disillusioned. Hitler was particularly distrustful of those who professed to be his friends. And he was known to despise collaborators more than most.

Norway fights back

Grim times tend to give rise to gallows humour. In Norway during the German occupation, there were few reasons to smile, but the people found ways to keep their spirits up and kick back at the Germans without fear of reprisals.

In April 1940, the Wehrmacht goose-stepped through Oslo in triumph, while the inhabitants watched with heavy hearts – well, all but one old lady, who berated a Nazi officer for his arrogance and for not tipping his hat to her, so she knocked it off with her cane. Incredibly, he apologized and rejoined the parade. It was the fourth hat she had knocked off that morning.

While the serious business of sabotage and assassination was carried out by the 40,000 members of Milorg, the Norwegian resistance, a further 15,000 Norwegian civilians did their part by contributing to and distributing some of the 30,000 underground newspapers and leaflets that informed the fact-starved population. Their contents were obtained from listening to the exiled government broadcasting on the BBC, an act prohibited by the Germans and punishable by death.

The Norwegians suffered food shortages and travel restrictions just as their neighbours did in the other occupied territories, but the Norwegians were also subjected to ludicrous attempts by the Nazis to convince them that they shared a mythical Aryan origin and it was this which generated some of the ridicule. The Nazi propaganda ministry worked overtime producing spurious theories to support their racial ideology, including the fanciful notion that the Hitler salute had originated with the Vikings.

The population took to wearing red as a symbol of their national identity and greeting each other with 'Merry Norwegian Christmas' to stress their independence and national pride. The Germans demonstrated their intolerance for even the smallest act of defiance by confiscating items of red clothing worn in public. This gave rise to a national joke that had visitors to police headquarters asking for directions to the dress department.

Diaries of defiance

Fraternization with Norwegian women was encouraged by the Nazi authorities, who hoped that it might lead to more Aryan children to swell the ranks of the SS. Himmler's elite were urged to participate in the state-sanctioned *Lebensborn* racial breeding programme and the Wehrmacht rank and file were urged to seduce Norwegian women at every opportunity.

As a result, girls and women were propositioned in public; whether they were with a man or alone, it did not deter the predatory soldiers. Women were followed and, if they resisted, threatened with imprisonment. Many were raped with no recourse to the law. The Norwegian civil courts had no jurisdiction over the occupation forces and the SS were immune from prosecution, even in German courts.

Historian Loni Klara cites just one of the countless incidents recorded in private journals and diaries by terrified, defenceless girls: that of the diarist, Cecilie Schou-Sorensen of Oslo. Schou-Sorensen described a nurse (herself perhaps) pursued by a German soldier who followed her home in the evening. She managed to reach her front door and get inside before he could catch her, but the next day she received a notice ordering her to report and apologize or face three months in prison.

Keeping a diary was a punishable offence, as many journals recorded the writer's hatred for the Germans. So the writers had to be as resourceful in hiding them as they would a radio or underground newspaper. Even their private thoughts when written down were seen as treasonable by the regime.

The Norwegians were so desperate to express their loathing for their oppressors that even the smallest and seemingly insignificant acts were seen as a victory, though such acts risked severe reprisals. Editors of the heavily censored Norwegian language newspapers inserted deliberate errors whenever possible to ridicule the authorities, whose grasp of the language was rudimentary at best.

Loni Klara gives two typical examples: the editor who listed the winners of a fictitious ski competition, whose initials spelt out the Norwegian equivalent of 'God Damn Hitler' and another who wrote that the Germans were superior in men and rabbits ('*menn og kaniner*') when he had been instructed to write men and cannons ('*menn og kanoner*').

A Norwegian cold shoulder

The safest and most common form of defiance was simply to cold-shoulder the Germans. Public transport was the primary source of travel to and from work since private cars were uncommon and petrol was rationed and restricted. Civilians and soldiers shared trams and trains, but a Norwegian would stand rather than sit next to a German soldier, even if there was no other seat available. The practice became so common that the authorities issued notices prohibiting passengers from standing when there was a free seat.

DENMARK – 9 April 1940

The Danes had capitulated on 9 April 1940 after only a few hours of sporadic fighting, the Danish government fearing that there would be needless deaths and destruction if the army continued a hopeless fight against overwhelming odds.

Having inflicted few casualties on the enemy and surrendered quickly, the Danes were initially treated comparatively leniently by their new German masters, who hoped for an alliance with those they considered their Aryan brothers.

The Danish Nazi Party was a vociferous presence in parliament, but senior Danish politicians hoped they would remain a minority with little influence if the government appeared willing to co-operate with the regime. The Danes were consequently allowed to govern themselves, administering the occupation's edicts under the watchful eye of SS General Werner Best.

Although the population endured blackouts, rationing, shortages and travel restrictions, they were able to resume their lives without too much interference from the occupation forces. But while there were many Danes who understood their government's attitude, there were those who loathed the Nazis and all that they stood for. These men and women organized themselves into underground units, distributing anti-German leaflets and newspapers and conducting acts of sabotage, targeting factories that had been taken over by the Germans for the manufacture of armaments and military equipment as well as the Danish companies who were producing material for the Wehrmacht.

As these attacks increased, relations deteriorated quickly and the Germans came to distrust the Danish civil administration, whom they suspected of harbouring the resistance and offering its members more than just moral support.

The resistance fighters were sensitive to their countrymen's opposition to violence on principle and so staged non-violent protests, including raids on cinemas during which they projected caricatures of Hitler while playing pre-recorded anti-Nazi speeches to the audience. Those underground were even prepared to use precious explosives to salute the birth of Princess Benedikte on 29 April 1944 in a Copenhagen park. Such action was intended to demonstrate that the resistance was loyal to the monarchy, even though many resistance members were communists.

The Germans were also incensed by the Danes' unwillingness to implement anti-Jewish policies and by the protection given to Danish Jews by the country's civil courts, which had imprisoned two editors of a National Socialist weekly, the *Battle Sign*, for anti-Semitic libel in May 1942.

Denmark – the cost of co-operation

The Nazis had hoped that Denmark would serve as a model protectorate, an example of peaceful collaboration that might encourage other countries to lay down their arms, roll over and join Hitler's New Order. But the Danes were not as compliant as the arrogant Germans had assumed they would be. They had not capitulated because they wished to ally themselves with the Third Reich and share the spoils of war with their 'Aryan' brothers, but only because they wished to spare Copenhagen from the punitive destruction that had been meted out to Rotterdam and Warsaw.

Within two years the Germans would be looking over their shoulders, acutely aware that they were unwelcome interlopers in a hostile land. A 1943 report in the *Saturday Evening Post* suggested that the peaceful Danes had been willing to compromise to ensure their peaceful existence, but that was not to say that they were docile or subservient. In the months following the invasion on 9 April 1940, the Danes exhibited a stoicism that the occupying forces mistakenly assumed was consent. But they were struggling with their conscience, asking themselves if perhaps they ought to have put up a fight, for their failure to do so had isolated them from their European neighbours and left many with a bitter taste in the mouth.

A dozen or so Danes had died on that first morning while their leaders argued and since then their countrymen had wondered if the world thought they lacked courage. As a tearful Dane told the *Post* reporter, 'We've kept our flag and our government and we haven't been bombed, but we are going to envy those Danish soldiers who are dead.'

The Danish Nazi Party

Capitulation had dealt a mortal blow to the pride of the Danish, whose fierce warrior ancestors had crossed the seas to plunder and trade as far as North America, the Near East and Novgorod (Russia). Having surrendered, they were then forced to stand idly by while Norway, the Netherlands, France, Belgium and Britain fought on.

As a Danish journalist confessed to the *Post*, 'When I think of my wife, I am glad we did not fight. But what of my son? What will he think when he is grown? What will he read in the world's history books of the part Denmark played?'

They had stuck to their pacifist principles, but at the cost of their self-respect.

The Danish stubbornly resisted the Nazis' attempts to indoctrinate them with racist ideology and turned a deaf ear to pernicious propaganda; in doing so, they demonstrated that the experiment had failed. As the *Post* noted, 'They listened to the Nazis and read what the Nazis had to say, and turned it all aside with quiet contempt.'

They mocked the Danish Nazi Party and cold-shouldered the Germans on the street, in cafés and restaurants and put a safe distance between themselves and the invader, even on overcrowded public transport. They shunned those who socialized with Germans and when Hitler was mentioned in conversation or when his speeches were broadcast on the radio, the Danes made a point of replying, 'Who is that?' to express their wilful disregard for the Führer. They had not suffered the restrictions imposed by the Germans on the citizens of other occupied countries. They could listen to foreign broadcasts and their underground press operated more freely with copies being delivered by the regular mail.

The Churchill Club

Resistance was low-key and more symbolic than anything. A group of Danish youths formed a group, which called itself the Churchill Club, to steal items belonging to German soldiers. The most prized item was a helmet, but some managed to purloin a bayonet. Those who were caught would be arrested by the Danish police, only to escape during the night when their guards neglected to lock the cell door.

More worrying for the Germans was the establishment of a Danish Youth Organization, Dansk Ungdomssamvirke, which was formed to celebrate Danish nationalism and the heroes who drove the Germans out of Denmark in the 14th century. Meanwhile, their parents' generation expressed its loathing for the Nazis by every means at their disposal. Shipyard workers complained that the recently built pier was unsafe and downed tools while their union demanded an exhaustive inspection, which took an inordinately long time. Construction was halted on the main airfield while workers and supervisors negotiated over extra pay for the many hours of sleep their workmen lost due to low-flying Allied aircraft. When news spread that a captured Allied airman was being held in a Danish hospital, the patient received hundreds of floral tributes from local well-wishers. The Germans decreed that only one bouquet would be allowed in future, so the next time an Allied pilot was captured, a truck pulled up to the hospital where he was being held. On board was a single giant bouquet comprising hundreds of small floral tributes which had been bound together. And when a downed RAF bomber pilot was paraded through the streets of Copenhagen under armed guard, he was not berated by an angry mob for dropping bombs on the city, but showered with flowers.

Butter and bacon

Acts of sabotage amounted to no more than a few isolated incidents, but they showed the Germans that they could not afford to be complacent.

Trains were derailed, factory workshops were subject to arson attacks and industrial machinery was intentionally disabled. Some fires were attributed to faulty wiring and acts of God, but the Germans would tolerate only so much delay. In the first three years of the occupation, 3,000 Danes were imprisoned for various 'anti-German' acts.

But while the ordinary Dane did whatever he or she could in the way of showing passive resistance, their government continued to placate their oppressor, dispatching Foreign Minister Erik Scavenius to Berlin to reassure Hitler of his compatriots' unfaltering loyalty.

And what did the Germans get from Denmark? As much butter and bacon as they could ship back to Berlin: one and a half million pigs and 13 million chickens, plus property to the value of two and a half billion crowns. The Germans also shipped 42,000 able-bodied Danes off to Germany to work in the factories, though they left the farmers at liberty and paid them handsomely for their produce and livestock. But they did not win the hearts and minds of the Danes. No matter how compliant the Danes appeared, they were not going to become pawns in Hitler's model protectorate.

Taking to the streets

With news of the first defeats for Germany on the Eastern Front in 1943, young Danes took to the streets to engage in armed attacks on German soldiers. That summer, strikes and demonstrations were organized in major towns and cities, beginning in Esbjerg and Odense and quickly spreading across the country, seeing workers clash with Danish police.

After the Danish government refused to implement the death penalty for sabotage, the Germans imposed a state of emergency on 29 August and shut down the parliament. They disarmed the Danish army and attempted to seize sea-worthy vessels. These were deliberately sunk by the navy to prevent them from being used against the Allies.

Matters reached a critical point in October after a German embassy attaché, Georg Duckwitz, informed a Danish politician of a planned round-up of Jews. All but 485 of Denmark's 8,000 Jews were sheltered by those opposed to Nazi racial policy and subsequently shipped to neutral Sweden, where they survived the war.

Incensed by what they saw as Danish interference, the Germans imposed further restrictions on the population and threatened reprisals for acts of sabotage and spreading anti-German propaganda.

This only incited more acts of defiance by a population emboldened by news of the Allied invasion of France in June 1944. For the last six months of the occupation, there were several major strikes by Danish workers. The possibility that the Danish police might join them was a threat that the Germans could not risk and so they disbanded the police, leaving the country under martial law. But on 4 May 1945, before the situation reached a crisis, the Germans surrendered, despite the fact that not a single Allied soldier had crossed the border to liberate the Danes.

Terrorism and resistance

In every country occupied by the Nazis and their allies, there was a degree of armed resistance as well as non-violent opposition. More than 70 years after the end of the Second World War, the guerrilla war waged against the Nazis is frequently cited as justification for acts of terror by those opposed to a political administration or an occupying force with which they do not agree. But resistance in time of war and terrorism are two distinctly different things.

By definition, terrorism refers to a campaign of indiscriminate violence designed to create a climate of fear among the general population, whereas violent acts of resistance during the Second World War were aimed at specific targets, namely the occupying forces and their collaborators.

Danish resistance was arguably unique, in that it took a non-violent form as a matter of principle to avoid collateral damage to property and civilian casualties. Unlike the Yugoslavian and Greek partisans, the Danes resisted calls to form guerrilla groups and chose non-violent means, because violence was considered to be contrary to their culture.

The Danish response to German occupation was largely determined by the conduct of the occupation forces and the passive collaboration of the Danish government. Unlike Norway, there was no attempt to Germanize the Danes, as they were considered to be of Aryan origin, nor were there incidents of widespread atrocities to incite insurgents, as was the case in Eastern Europe.

The Night and Fog Decree

Denmark was not officially at war with Nazi Germany. It remained neutral, having capitulated after only a few hours during which 16 of its soldiers had been killed. Its cities were spared the punitive bombing which had been dealt out to Rotterdam and Warsaw and the Danish government settled for a diplomatic protest in response to the invasion. Germany's occupation was primarily a strategic move, as it needed a bridgehead in Scandinavia, rather than a full-scale invasion to enslave the population and plunder the nation's resources, as had been the case elsewhere. Germany also required the co-operation of Danish farmers, fishermen and factories, who were to supply ten per cent of the Reich's annual consumption of meat and butter, 11 per cent of its sugar and 18 per cent of its fish.

In return for their swift capitulation, the Danes were guaranteed their political independence. Their king and parliament remained in place, while the police, the judiciary and public institutions continued to function as before under Danish control. But to maintain their non-belligerent status and appease their uninvited 'guests', the Danish government made it known that they would not tolerate any acts of defiance against the Germans for fear of angering them.

The Communist Party of Denmark was banned in August 1941 and its members arrested. Hotels, cafés and bars were prohibited from tuning their radios to the BBC and other Allied stations, although private homes were not subject to the ban on foreign broadcasts. In addition, anti-German art, dramatic works, films and literature were banned so as not to offend the occupation. Schools and higher education institutions were instructed to deter pupils and students from attending anti-German protests and church leaders were ordered to avoid preaching sermons against the occupation and to remove any inflammatory material from their parish publications.

In return, Hitler made an exception for the Danes when drawing up the Night and Fog Decree in December 1941, which called for the arrest and imprisonment without trial of suspected resistance members and their summary execution. Nevertheless, 102 members of the Danish resistance were executed during the occupation – 65 of these in the last three months of the war.

Resistance builds

It suited the Germans to have such a passive and co-operative country, for they only needed a token force of two reserve divisions and few more than 200 officials to control the population of four million. As a consequence, the Danish resistance, which consisted in the main of members of the banned Communist Party and adolescent boys, had a freer hand than their counterparts in other occupied countries, having to contend with a smaller contingent of German security forces. But they did not enjoy the support of the vast majority of the Danish people, who were said to have approved the government's policy of collaboration. For that reason, the underground movement limited its activities to disrupting communication and transport, committing arson attacks on factories and businesses owned by or operating primarily for the Germans and the distribution of anti-Nazi propaganda. If they had graduated to assassinating German soldiers, they might have lost public support and that of their own government, at a time when the nation was entirely dependent on Germany for much of its raw materials.

Denmark was able to obtain supplies of coal, oil and minerals from Germany after its lifeline to Britain had been cut. But while the Danes were spared deportation to forced labour camps and factories in the Reich as well as the constant threat of arrest and imprisonment without trial, as was the case in other occupied countries, the Germans, as ever, were not content with what they had. They demanded more and more in terms of productivity, imposed longer working hours, placed more restrictions on freedom of movement and increased rationing until the population spilled out on to the streets to protest in August 1943, bringing industry to a standstill and forcing the government out of office. It is thought that a tenth of the population took part in the strikes. The best the remaining civil servants could do was to press the Germans to allow Danish prisoners to receive Red Cross parcels and to spare deported Danish Jews from the gas chambers.

The propaganda war

Prior to August 1943, anti-German feeling was limited to mass gatherings to commemorate Danish historical figures and the communal singing of patriotic songs to demonstrate unity and opposition to National Socialist policy.

After 1943, the resistance enjoyed increasing popular support and was provided with arms and explosives by the SOE in London. There was a feeling that the war was turning against the aggressor, with defeats on the Russian Front and the fall of Mussolini which had effectively left Nazi Germany fighting alone on two fronts in Europe. Incidents of sabotage escalated, but the purpose was not so much to harass the enemy as to influence public opinion against any form of co-operation with the enemy. The resistance was then seen as the legitimate voice and will of the Danish nation and the government was discredited. The operation to save Danish Jews in October 1943 marked a significant turning point in the occupation and it saw a dramatic increase in the number of active resistance groups.

By the spring of 1944, there were more than 15,000 actively engaged in the resistance with a substantial number comprising the core of the underground army. By the following spring, this force had grown to 50,000, or six per cent of the male population. Young girls and women also participated, though they were mainly involved in distributing food, clothing and propaganda leaflets, hiding weapons and explosives and assisting Allied airmen to safety.

But the primary weapon of the Danish resistance was propaganda. At one point there were 550 different papers with a total circulation of 55 million. Some of them were little more than pamphlets, while others were broadsheets running to several pages. This reached a peak in the closing months of the war, when the total circulation of these sheets reached three million copies a month. Their content comprised uncensored news sourced from the BBC, the naming of collaborators and calls for specific action on targets in urban areas where the underground army was active.

The argument for sabotage

The Danish underground was unique in seeking the approval of the workers who would be affected by their acts of sabotage. As early as the spring of 1942, the Communists asked employees at several major industrial plants if they were willing to offer their support for acts of sabotage that might bring reprisals. The majority were in favour, regardless of the consequences. In the summer of 1943, a group calling itself The Circle polled 1,300 Danes from diverse backgrounds to gauge their opinion on the same subject and discovered a resounding 70 per cent endorsed sabotage as a legitimate means of resistance. The argument centred on sabotage as a means of saving lives, both as a result of disrupting the production of weapons used by Germany and as means of reducing the collateral damage and casualties from Allied air raids. If the Danes put key factories, railway depots and other military installations out of action, then the Allies were less likely to risk losing the pilots sent to bomb them.

This argument was particularly effective, as it reminded the Danes of a British air raid on the Copenhagen shipyards in January 1943, when the nearby residential area was accidently bombed resulting in 3,400 people being made homeless. In December that year, a Danish resistance group, BOPA, sabotaged a power station at the same shipyard with no loss of life or damage to adjacent houses. The same group was responsible for the single act of terrorism carried out by the Danes during the entire occupation – the bombing of Café Mokka in Copenhagen on 27 October 1943. This café was a popular meeting place frequented by German soldiers. Its bombing was an isolated act of revenge for the torture and murder of BOPA member Aage Nielsen by the Gestapo and had not been sanctioned by the leadership, which felt obligated to denounce it in the underground press.

But the main argument in favour of sabotage was that the Danes were obliged to do whatever they could to defeat Nazism, which was anti-democratic and repressive. Moreover, having accommodated the Nazis initially, Denmark had to demonstrate its opposition to tyranny in no uncertain terms before it was condemned by the Allies and its neighbours as a collaborationist. It had acted as a servant of the Nazi state by legitimizing informants and declaring that anyone who had information regarding the resistance was obliged to notify the authorities. Refusal to do so would be 'acting contrary to the interests of his country', according to a speech by Social Democratic Prime Minister Vilhelm Buhl on 2 September 1942. Prime Minister Buhl pledged that his government would prosecute those accused of sabotage and other crimes against the Wehrmacht, an announcement which angered members of the resistance, who viewed this as betrayal.

Terror and counter-terror

The fine line between co-operation and collaboration was breached when the Danish government passed a law on 4 December 1942 that permitted the employment of armed guards at key industrial sites to deter saboteurs. Early in the new year, the Ministry of Justice informed the country's senior police officers that combatting sabotage was critical to national security and that they were to make the fight against sabotage a priority by supplying factory guards with guns. When in the last weeks of 1942 the regular police proved unwilling to implement 'anti-terrorist' measures and unable to make sufficient arrests to satisfy their German supervisors, the Germans brought in the Gestapo. Immediately the rate of arrests increased to 169 for specific acts of sabotage and 424 for other illegal activities.

But the Gestapo were chasing shadows. No sooner had their agents infiltrated and neutralized one cell than another formed, as new recruits replaced those who had been arrested. And with each action the resistance grew more wary, more secretive and more cunning, protecting each cell by keeping it independent of the others.

Werner Best, the German plenipotentiary in Denmark and Günther Pancke, the head of the German police, advocated the slow, systematic elimination of each resistance group and the prosecution of its members in a court of law, but Hitler was impatient for results. He told Best, 'Terror can only be fought with counter-terror.'

A campaign of murder

On 30 December 1943, Hitler appointed Otto Bovensiepen chief of the German Security Police and entrusted him with implementing a campaign of indiscriminate terror. In 1944, his powers were extended to Denmark. Danish shops, factories, places of entertainment and the editorial offices of Danish newspapers were targeted in arson and bomb attacks by squads of both German and Danish Nazis, in acts designed to demoralize and intimidate. Suspected members of the resistance, their families and their friends were rounded up, interrogated and executed, their names published alongside the names of informers who had been assassinated by the resistance, so as to imply that the murders were in retaliation. It is believed that 600 Danes were murdered during this campaign.

Best issued an ultimatum to the resistance, offering to commute the death sentences of convicted 'saboteurs' (i.e. those accused of illegal acts in Nazi courts) if the incidents of sabotage were reduced. But the Danes were not to be blackmailed in this way and abhorred the idea that their friends were being held hostage, so they continued their campaign against German military targets and premises owned by Danish Nazis.

Second wave of strikes

By the summer of 1944, there could be no doubting the public mood and its vehement opposition to the Germans. A second wave of strikes erupted in Copenhagen in protest against German reprisals to a BOPA attack on an arms factory. The Germans had executed eight alleged saboteurs and demolished key public places in the city before banning all public gatherings and imposing a curfew.

Shipyard workers were the first to walk out, followed by factory workers and office staff. Barricades were set up all over the city. Shops and businesses owned by Danish Nazis were vandalized and at the height of the protests, it seemed as if the vast majority of Copenhagen's citizens were on the streets after dark in defiance of the curfew.

The Germans cut off supplies of electricity, water and gas and unleashed the Schalburg Corps, a Danish Nazi paramilitary group, to break up the crowds. It is believed that 100 protestors were killed in violent clashes with these thugs and more than 600 wounded. But the Germans eventually conceded defeat, lifting the curfew and redeploying the Schalburg Corps outside the city.

There would be other protests against executions of saboteurs, deportations and the internment of the Danish police, but as the occupation dragged on, the public's appetite for strikes and protests waned. It was clear the war was winding down and the Germans would soon be pulling out. No one wanted to incite them to take reprisals of the kind they had heard about in Poland and Czechoslovakia.

Hitler's bloodlust would not be satiated. On 30 July 1944, having suffered loss of face in Denmark, he issued the 'Terror and Sabotage Decree', which ordered the summary execution of all saboteurs in all the occupied countries and relieved the courts of prosecuting offenders.

Assassination

Following the execution of resistance members in the winter of 1943, the Freedom Council (the leadership of the Danish resistance movement) debated the merits of assassinating German officers, but decided against it for several reasons. The main argument against taking such action was of course the risk of fierce reprisals, but another was the belief that the officers' replacements might be even worse. Furthermore, such actions would be against 'the Danish conception of Justice'. They had the opportunity to assassinate the Reichskommissar for Norway, Josef Terboven, during a visit to Copenhagen, but the proposal was defeated by a single vote, the argument being that the Danes would be unwilling to suffer the reprisals incurred for the eradication of a single Nazi and one whose fate would not otherwise affect Denmark.

But the growing resentment felt by many within the resistance movement towards the Germans prompted some to advocate the arbitrary shooting of ordinary German soldiers and the taking of officers as hostages in exchange for the resistance fighters who faced execution. Even then, the Freedom Council issued a strong condemnation of such practices on the grounds that these were the very same methods used by the Nazis. Only informers were to be 'neutralized', indeed 343 are known to have been killed. These killings would be seen as political murders and justified as acts of self-defence. But even these had to be sanctioned by the leadership, so acutely sensitive were they to possible accusations of engaging in terrorism. Many informers were exiled to Sweden under the threat of being assassinated should they seek to return.

The extent to which the Danes had turned from co-operating with the occupation to openly defying it can be determined by the number of its citizens interned as political prisoners in German concentration camps or in the Danish internment camp at Frøslev. One quarter of the population, 10,000 Danes, had forfeited their freedom to protest against the German occupation and hundreds, perhaps thousands, more had died defying the dictator.

LUXEMBOURG – 10 May 1940

For many high-ranking officers of the Wehrmacht, the euphoria of their swift victory over France and the Low Countries was tempered by the realization that it had been won not for Germany, but for the regime. As one senior commander told a Luxembourg citizen, 'You may think it's pretty bad to have the German army here at all, but wait until the bandits and gangsters of the Nazi Party are put in control, and you will wish that you had the German army to maintain order and protect you!'

To the regular soldiers, the Nazi Party officials who were to form the administration in the occupied countries were commonly known as 'scum and rabble' ('*Pack und Gesindel*').

Whatever criticism may have been levelled at the Grand Duchess in the days after she left the country with members of her cabinet was soon replaced by widespread support for her decision, as it ensured the legitimacy of her government in exile.

In her place, the Nazis enthroned Gustav Simon, the gauleiter of Koblenz, who had been described by Luxembourg's American Consul, George Waller, as 'a swinish bully', brutal, ignorant, stubborn and vain.

His civil administration was attended by 'a swarm of Gestapo, an army of spies, informers, agents, provocateurs' and a multitude of party members hoping to advance their careers and profit from the occupation. If there wasn't a post for each of these parasites, one would be created.

The middle-aged Simon was typical of the lowly party official who found themselves entrusted with the lives of millions when the Wehrmacht pulled out or were redeployed elsewhere.

Having failed to pass the exams required to become an elementary school teacher, he committed himself to the National Socialist cause. After embezzling funds, he avoided imprisonment and possibly execution by threatening to expose secrets that would bring down senior members of the Nazi Party, which he had arranged to be made public in the event of his death. In return for his silence, Simon was made gauleiter and no questions were raised when he built himself a palace fit for a monarch.

Double-speak and monkey talk

The Nazi takeover of Luxembourg's civil administration was done with typical German thoroughness and efficiency and justified with characteristic Nazi double-speak. The Reich proclaimed that it was establishing a civil administration so that the country 'might no longer suffer from military government, but have the advantages of peacetime civil administration'.

However, Simon's government soon revealed its true intentions by outlawing the French language, or as Simon crudely put it in his inauguration speech, 'French monkey talk'. Even the name of the country was erased now that it was assimilated into the Reich. He also dissolved parliament, outlawed all political parties and organizations other than the Nazi Party and confiscated all money and property belonging to those parties, making himself a wealthy man overnight.

'I want and have the means to get,' he told the assembled press, 'joyful compliance with all my laws and decrees and eager co-operation in speeding up my Germanification of this misguided country.'

Simon enthroned himself in the marble palace that had been built for the Luxembourg Steel Trust, while the Gestapo requisitioned a grand villa owned by a prominent physician. The latter was soon notorious for the screams and cries of torture victims emanating from the basement cells.

us in a truck and you're gone. You can't even tell your family you've gone. Yes, it's a world of fear. That's what we were so afraid of – to be taken.'

Nelly and her two older sisters were sent away to live with her aunt in Charleroi, far from the fighting on the Belgian–German border. Her schoolteacher parents were ordered to remain behind in their posts until the Germans invaded. They followed on foot, taking six weeks to complete the journey and enduring attacks by the German fighters who flew over the streams of refugees, machine-gunning the civilians to spread panic and blocking the roads for retreating Allied troops and vehicles.

But the joy of being reunited was soon offset by the fear of German occupation and the privations that followed.

Every year was worse than the last. 'Nobody was fat in those days,' Nelly remembered. 'Some children really were starving.'

Jozefina Vedts

Jozefina Vedts was 13 when the Germans came to her village of Haacht in the province of Brabant. She was the youngest of ten children. Three of her older brothers were already fighting with the army.

The Germans measured the Vedts' land and instructed the family on what crops they could grow and how much they would have to 'donate' to the Reich. When the family's chickens failed to provide the required number of eggs, they were forced to make up the shortfall by buying them on the black market. The Germans would not accept that the chickens had failed to be productive and accused the family of having eaten them. It was dangerous to deceive the Germans, but families were often so desperate that they had to take the chance or starve. The Vedts kept two pigs and they managed to keep the existence of the second pig a secret from the Germans.

When Jozefina was 14, she enrolled at a school in Brussels to train as a seamstress. Her journey of 15 miles (24 km) by tram required her to obtain a travel permit. If she couldn't produce it, she could be arrested and forced to work for the Germans. The trams were always subject to being stopped and searched and Jozefina witnessed many passengers being forcibly taken, never to be seen again. Allied bombing meant that every journey was fraught with danger, especially at the point where it passed the airport, a favourite target of the Allied planes.

As German officers and their administrative staff travelled by tram, the civilians were restricted to one part of the carriage which was invariably overcrowded and where young women often found themselves being propositioned.

Like many of their fellow Belgians, the Vedts enjoyed a belated revenge on their oppressors when the Germans retreated in 1945 leaving behind their warm military overcoats and other useful articles that could be utilized by deprived civilians.

THE NETHERLANDS – 14 May 1940

> 'Nations of heroes do not exist. But there were among the Dutch tens of thousands of ordinary human beings, men and women, who did save the country's soul.'
>
> Louis de Jong, Dutch historian

14 May 1940 was a typical spring day in the Netherlands, warm, cloudless and sunny, but a storm was gathering. In the skies, the screaming Stuka dive bombers were massing for a devastating strike on Rotterdam. The second largest city in Holland was a strategic port and its systematic destruction was intended to shock the Dutch into surrendering.

Hitler had boasted that he would conquer the Netherlands in a single day, but after four days of intense fighting, his generals conceded they had met stiff resistance and couldn't break the stalemate. Incensed, Hitler ordered the Luftwaffe to destroy Rotterdam, as a warning of what would happen if the Dutch did not capitulate.

The centre of the city was levelled and 800 civilians were killed. Many more would have perished had the city not been evacuated in anticipation of the bombing. The threat of further bombing on other towns and cities forced the Dutch to surrender.

The question was then whether to continue as if nothing had changed, co-operate with the occupation forces or actively oppose the enemy – *Aanpassen, meedoen, of verzetten* ('adjust, collaborate or resist?').

The Dutch, who had remained neutral in the First World War, were opposed in principle to a regime which restricted their freedom and which would deny them their democratic rights. They would not be dictated to or forced to obey the will of one man and so had no choice but to resist, either actively with violence or passively by not co-operating. Diverse groups made their unwillingness to co-operate known from the first weeks of the occupation. Farmers refused to pay tribute, artists declined to join the German Chamber of Culture although it meant loss of work and many doctors rejected demands for them to become members of the German Medical Association or to implement Nazi racial theories. Some chose to give up practice rather than give in to German demands. Others were forced into hiding, sheltered by a group of fellow physicians who formed an underground organization to offer sanctuary to their own.

Dutch opposition to the Nazi race laws was supported by the Catholic and Reformed Churches, who issued a pastoral letter to all members of their congregation urging civil disobedience to what they condemned as immoral laws.

A new Netherlands in a new Europe

Initially, the Germans made an effort to appear affable, in the hope that the Dutch would accept their presence and might even be persuaded to subscribe to National Socialist doctrines.

The Germans did not impose martial law in Holland, as they had done in Poland and Czechoslovakia. Nor did they install their own officials to administer the country. Instead, they allowed the civil authorities to remain in place to oversee the process of Dutch law.

The Germans unleashed an extensive campaign to win over the population with posters, film screenings and radio broadcasts extolling the virtues of the New Order and the desirability of ridding Europe in general and Holland in particular of 'undesirable' elements, specifically Jews, Romany people, Slavs, Jehovah's Witnesses, communists and homosexuals.

The posters were everywhere inviting the Dutch to join the New Order and create 'a new Netherlands in a new Europe'.

They managed to convince a large number to join the Dutch Nazi Party, the NSB, and its youth organization by appealing to their nationalism and their vanity with the argument that white Europeans shared a common Aryan root stock and, as such, were members of a superior race.

NSB mass meetings attracted fervent supporters, who were promised important roles in the regime, for the Germans knew that to subjugate a population they had to recruit collaborators who would control, supervise and inform on those who refused to conform. The Germans could not simply occupy a densely populated country of nine million and police the population unless they had allies within who would monitor those whom they wanted to subjugate and control.

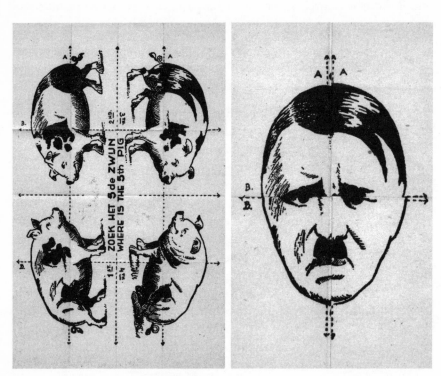

A subversive puzzle from occupied Holland, but the kind of item that could have cost its owner his or her life if the Gestapo were to find it. The question, 'Where is the 5th PIG?', is answered by making the correct folds in the picture of the four pigs to get the rather satisfying result on the right.

But the majority of the Dutch people viewed the NSB as traitors. The Netherlands became divided into those who despised the Nazis and were resistant to indoctrination, and those who were seen as betraying the country's way of life to further their own ends as pawns of the Nazi Party.

Although the attendance at these rallies may have pleased their Nazi masters, it only amounted to fewer than 2 per cent of the population – 98 per cent of the nation remained resistant to propaganda.

Street-fighting men

The NSB organized a paramilitary wing modelled on Hitler's storm troopers or 'Brown-shirts'. These thugs assaulted Jews and other 'enemies of the state' in the streets and vandalized Jewish-owned shops and homes, with the approval of their Nazi puppet masters. But the Dutch would not stand by and allow their fellow citizens to be beaten and humiliated. They formed anti-Nazi vigilante groups called *Knokploegen* ('Fighting units') and engaged both the Dutch Nazis and their German cronies in open warfare on the streets of Amsterdam.

But there was no co-ordinated resistance movement. Two groups called for armed resistance – the Guezen Action Committee in Amsterdam and an affiliation of union leaders, underground newspaper publishers and resistance fighters calling themselves The Core – the former appealed in the early weeks of the occupation and the latter at its end, but neither were able to inflict significant damage on the enemy.

There was a willingness to fight the Germans, but the Dutch were hampered in their efforts to organize attacks, as they lacked the expertise and logistical support offered to the underground in other countries by the SOE. This British-based espionage and sabotage unit were unable to parachute agents into Holland due to the flat, open terrain and the presence of anti-aircraft batteries throughout the Netherlands. A sea landing was impossible due to the proliferation of German defences. When British agents managed to get through, they were immediately arrested by the Gestapo, who had been sending false messages since March 1942 using codes obtained from a captured SOE wireless operator.

It came down to spontaneous acts of defiance by individuals, the refusal to comply with Nazi edicts by various groups of professionals and organized strikes by students and manual workers to galvanize the population into demonstrating their opposition to the occupation and its policies.

Small acts of defiance

A truer picture of public apathy towards Nazi indoctrination can be gleaned from the mass demonstrations of public sympathy for the Dutch royal family. Orange carnations were worn on 29 June, Prince Bernhard's birthday, and vases of carnations were placed in shop windows and in the windows of private houses. A statue of Queen Wilhelmina's mother was also covered in carnations, prompting the outraged German authorities to arrest two of the organizers and a prominent Dutch general, Winkelman, who had taken no part in the protest but whose arrest was intended to demonstrate that no one would be immune from Nazi justice.

However, small acts of defiance continued. It became common practice to wear coins as jewellery, as they showed the image of the queen. Postage stamps were affixed to the upper left corner of envelopes and packages, leaving the upper right corner free as a sign of respect for their exiled monarch, who had fled to Britain in 1940 and whose image would normally have been placed there.

Seemingly innocuous acts also helped many to stick two fingers up at the enemy. Some took to raising their hats when the traffic lights changed to orange and hailed each other with the English-sounding greeting, 'Hallo', which was in fact an acronym for *Hang alle laffe landverraders op* ('Hang all cowardly traitors').

Banned from screening British and American films, cinemas were deserted, as German films were greeted with mass walk-outs and abuse. The Germans reacted by issuing new laws against such protests, but the Dutch simply stayed away. Instead, hundreds of thousands listened to the BBC, which, despite a ban, broadcast defiant messages from the Dutch government in exile; the Germans responded by confiscating every wireless set they could find.

The February Strike

There were small, spontaneous strikes throughout Holland during that first year of the occupation, the first of which had been staged by students at Leiden and other universities, in protest at the dismissal of Jewish professors. This was followed on 17 February 1941 by the ship-workers, who downed tools in protest against plans to send them to build naval vessels in Germany.

Amsterdam from her secret hiding place: an annex above her father's business premises in Prinsengracht. It was not written for publication or to impress or horrify, but merely to record her personal, intimate impressions of a life lived in fear of discovery. Tragically, her fears were well founded, for the family and their friends, the Van Pels, were betrayed to the Germans just months before the war ended and all were transported to Auschwitz. Only Otto Frank, Ann's father, survived.

Anne Frank at her desk, c.1941.

Anne was born in Frankfurt am Main in 1929 and might have remained there to marry and have a family of her own were it not for the fact that she was Jewish. The rise of the Nazis and their anti-Jewish laws made it impossible for her father to continue in business and so he took his wife, Edith, and two daughters, Anne and her elder sister Margot, to Holland. The family made every effort to fit in, learning the language and making friends, but on 10 May 1940, the German army invaded the Netherlands, forcing the Frank family into hiding to escape the round-ups, which were correctly rumoured to end in the gas chambers of Auschwitz and other extermination camps.

Just before the family went into hiding on 6 July 1942, Anne received a diary for her 13th birthday; for the next two years she confided her private thoughts and feelings in it. The simple act of keeping a diary was expressly forbidden in Nazi-occupied Europe. After an appeal was made on Radio Orange for all diarists to keep a record of events, she began to rewrite her entries as one continuous narrative.

As her diary entries for October 1942 reveal, the Franks and the wider Jewish community knew what awaited them, even if their non-Jewish neighbours were tempted to dismiss the stories as Allied propaganda.

> 9 October 1942
> Our many Jewish friends and acquaintances are being taken away in droves. The Gestapo is treating them very roughly and transporting them in cattle cars to Westerbork, the big camp in Drenthe to which they're sending all the Jews... The people get almost nothing to eat, much less to drink, as water is available only one hour a day, and there's only one toilet and sink for several thousand people... We assume that most of them are being murdered. The English radio says they're being gassed. Perhaps that's the quickest way to die.

The same day she recorded what was happening to her neighbours in retaliation for acts of resistance.

> Leading citizens – innocent people – are taken prisoner to await their execution. If the Gestapo can't find the

saboteur, they simply grab five hostages and line them up against the wall. You read the announcements of their death in the paper, where they're referred to as "fatal accidents."

Fine specimens of humanity, those Germans, and to think I'm actually one of them! No, that's not true, Hitler took away our nationality long ago.

On 13 January 1943, she witnessed the seemingly indiscriminate persecution of fellow Jews who had not been able to find a hiding place in time:

At any time of night and day, poor helpless people are being dragged out of their homes. They're allowed to take only a knapsack and a little cash with them, and even then, they're robbed of these possessions on the way. Families are torn apart; men, women and children are separated. Children come home from school to find that their parents have disappeared. Women return from shopping to find their houses sealed, their families gone. The Christians in Holland are also living in fear because their sons are being sent to Germany. Everyone is scared... The children in this neighbourhood run around in thin shirts and wooden shoes. They have no coats, no caps, no stockings and no one to help them. Gnawing on a carrot to still their hunger pangs, they walk from their cold houses through cold streets to an even colder classroom. Things have gotten so bad in Holland that hordes of children stop passers-by in the streets to beg for a piece of bread.

But on 4 August 1944, before she could complete her account, the family were betrayed and transported to Auschwitz. Anne and Margot were transported to Bergen-Belsen that November, where they both contracted typhus and died. Anne was just 15 years old.

FRANCE – 22 June 1940

Hearts and minds

> 'Never were we freer than under the German occupation. We had lost all our rights, and first of all our right to speak. They insulted us to our faces... They deported us *en masse*... And because of all this we were free... the occupation stripped human beings of their futures. Never again did we gaze after a young couple, attempting to imagine their destiny. We had no more destiny than a nail or a door knob.'
>
> Jean-Paul Sartre

Few Frenchmen had any conception of what life would be like following a defeat. Defeat itself was unimaginable for the victors of the First World War, who had put their faith in the impregnable Maginot Line, a formidable barrier of fortifications built across the north-east border with Germany. The Germans simply circumvented it by invading through Belgium in May 1940.

Having routed the once invincible French army and divided the defeated country to conserve their own forces, the Nazis attempted to win over the demoralized population by a combination of terror and flattery.

Many of the French were seduced by German assurances and impressed by the discipline of the Wehrmacht. Soldiers from the first German unit to march into Paris had been seen to wash the filth of battle from their faces and hands in the Canal de l'Ourcq in the Ile de France. Their officers had instructions to appear affable and courteous when requisitioning accommodation from the population, especially from the French aristocracy. According to French politician Pierre Mendès France, many of the bourgeoisie were not afraid to admit that they preferred Hitler to their socialist premier, Léon Blum, a view that was shared by a large proportion of the military leadership, who were drawn from the privileged class.

Under the jackboot

Pierre Mendès, who was a member of the pre-war government, recalled that in Bordeaux 'treason was everywhere', there was a 'will to surrender' and to accommodate the victors 'at any price'. Anglophobia and a 'horrible kind of cynicism' were rife. Pierre Laval blamed 'Anglo Saxon belligerence' for the continuation of the war. In July 1940, he told a colleague that as soon as the British saw sense and surrendered, the Germans would withdraw many of their troops from France and Pétain's government would convene in the capital where it would draft a new constitution.

People were quick to blame Premier Blum and the Popular Front, a left-wing, anti-fascist coalition which governed France in the 1930s, for the defeat and took out their anger by enacting 'petty revenge' on their own leaders, both in the immediate aftermath of the fall of France and well into the occupation. But the real reason for the defeat, according to British Foreign Secretary Anthony Eden, was Pétain's fear for the destruction of French cities, which led him to capitulate when there was still a chance of holding back the invader. Eden tried to convince Pétain that there were 'worse things than the destruction of town and cities', but the marshal was practically senile by this time and had no fight left in him. Incredibly, few blamed Pétain for giving in so soon and argued that the 'old man' had no other option.

Parisians were spared the destruction of their city by the swift surrender and France was spared a prolonged war of attrition. But now its people would be subjected to four years of living under the heel of the German jackboot and obeying orders imposed by the occupier.

Streets were deserted, there were hardly any cars on the roads, neon signs had been switched off and advertisements recalled a life that was now dead. As Jean-Paul Sartre observed, they 'seemed to be engraved on tombstones'.

In the immediate aftermath of the defeat, few Frenchmen and women knew what to do. The majority adopted a 'wait and see' attitude, according to Peter Fritzsche, a wavering from one day to the next, knowing that to commit to either passive co-operation or active resistance was fraught with dire consequences.

A cautious approach

Marcel Verdier, pharmacist in the town of Clermont-Ferrand, told documentary director Marcel Ophüls that in the immediate aftermath of the surrender 'the watchword was caution', because no one knew what their neighbours or even their own families felt about the Germans and so dare not speak their mind. The French press were under German control and no longer to be trusted, so many simply stopped reading the newspapers and concentrated on surviving.

Others began to openly adopt 'German values', to learn the language of the invader and express attitudes that they knew would be heard favourably by the authorities, namely virulently anti-Semitic views which had been dormant for decades but which were an undercurrent of a certain strata of French society. In Vichy, French officials greeted each other with the Hitler salute though, perversely, the zone refused to turn the clocks forward to German time, an adjustment deemed one step too many by the archly conservative French.

One of the first pamphlets circulated by the resistance in the summer of 1940 advised the French how to behave towards the enemy in their midst, as so many seemed uncertain what constituted collaboration and what small acts of civility would be permissible. Its author Jean Texcier reminded his fellow countrymen that the Germans were not tourists but conquerors and that they were not to be spoken to, even if they attempted to converse in French. Shops advertising the fact that 'German is spoken here' were to be boycotted and French radio and French newspapers avoided while they were under the control of the Germans. Oddly, the only interaction permitted was the lighting of a cigarette, as that was the one thing no one would refuse 'their worst enemy'.

'London' calling

Often the French were limited to token acts of resistance, tearing down or defacing German propaganda posters or chalking 'V for Victory' symbols and slogans on the walls. And they found strength in mass peaceful protests organized by their government in exile.

On Sunday 11 May 1940, to mark Joan of Arc day, 'London' – as the Free French radio was known – urged all Frenchmen and women to walk in the streets and greet each other openly. By doing so they would see themselves in others, as de Gaulle put it, and renew their sense of community. On New Year's Day 1941, 'London' called for an hour-long protest, which saw empty streets throughout France, as people stayed at home and drew their shutters. On 22 March, the French were instructed to write 'V for Victory' signs in public places to raise morale and demonstrate how widespread was the desire for victory over the enemy.

The Germans responded by imposing a Sunday curfew on adolescents, in the belief that teenagers were responsible for much of the graffiti and they instructed teachers to search their pupils' pockets for chalk.

Subtle but significant acts of co-operation, even collaboration, were evident to those affected by them. Pierre Mendès recalled that his wife and her best friend Madeleine were 'abused and insulted' by their own countrymen and that Madeleine, the wife of Popular Front politician Jean Zay, was refused admission to more than one maternity hospital because she was a Jew.

German time

France was the first occupied country to be ordered to conform to German time. This small but significant demand set the tone for the following four years of occupation as Germany asserted its dominance over its subjugated citizens outside its own borders. When the armistice was signed at 6.50 pm on 22 June, all the hour hands on all the clocks in France had been moved forward one hour in correspondence with Middle European Summer Time, as a wartime savings measure imposed by the victors.

As Peter Fritzsche wrote in *An Iron Wind*, this had the effect of forcing people out on to the streets in total darkness during winter mornings and confining them inside while the sun still burned bright in late summer evenings, whether curfews began at 10 pm and ended at 6 am or whether they were effective an hour further forward as they were later in the war. And if the resistance had been active, punitive curfews would be imposed to further restrict movement, such as when in December 1941, attacks on German soldiers in Paris saw the city locked down for days and the streets deserted after 6 pm.

Encouraging collaboration

The Germans declared that any acts of sabotage or armed resistance would be punished by brutal reprisals, the taking of hostages and the torture and execution of those responsible. At the same time, they attempted to seduce the population by appealing to hearts and minds.

After banning all French newspapers and periodicals, in January 1941, the Germans set up their own daily newspaper, *Pariser Zeitung*, a slim German language broadsheet with a supplement in French. Its primary purpose was to inform their own troops of the sights and

The French Third Republic and Nazi Germany signed an armistice ending the Battle of France in the Forest of Compiègne, 22 June 1940. The signing took place in the same railway carriage used to agree the armistice in 1918, but this time the boot was on the other foot. Adolf Hitler is second from the right.

sounds to be enjoyed in the French capital, but it was also hoped that the French would eventually be persuaded to see their new Nazi masters as allies in the struggle against communism and the mythical global Jewish conspiracy.

The *Pariser Zeitung*'s tone and content was rabidly anti-communist, anti-Semitic and anti-British, the latter intended to exploit the widely held feeling that the British had abandoned France to its fate after evacuating its own besieged troops at Dunkirk. Anti-British feelings still ran high and the Germans hoped to capitalize on this bitterness, while stressing the complementary nature of French and German culture. Collaboration was encouraged and French readers urged to think of collaboration as nothing to be ashamed of.

Pleasure in Paris

Paris was praised for its historical sights, its bustling boulevards, street cafés, nightclubs, its cuisine and its pretty women, while French businesses were encouraged to participate in fairs and exhibitions in France and in Germany. The implication was that if the French co-operated, they would profit from the New Order in Europe, while resistance would spoil the party for everyone. In this way, the occupying forces hoped to alienate the mass of the population from those stubborn individuals and groups who refused to admit defeat. Turning informer would be every Frenchman's duty to avoid 'unpleasantness'.

The paper's sycophantic fawning over French culture and cuisine sickened patriots who wished nothing more than to see the Boche march back to Berlin, but the fact was that the Germans were in France to stay, with the prospect of liberation merely wishful thinking.

The French were to consider themselves privileged to have been assimilated into the Third Reich and to now be under its protection. Paris was a pleasure garden, a centre for 'recreation and relaxation' as a British correspondent noted, to be enjoyed by all – if the French would agree to peaceful cohabitation.

Rumours abound

The German soldiers indulged themselves to excess, enjoying every attraction the City of Light had to offer. They set aside their racial ideology when it came to frequenting the brothels and nightclubs of Montmartre,

Parisians spend the first Bastille Day under Nazi occupation quietly.

where they were said to be particularly fond of the black prostitutes who had been imported from the French colonies. German officers were known to keep black mistresses in the district.

Parisians set aside their misgivings and read collaborationist periodicals such as *Le Matin*, the daily *Paris-Soir* and *Le Petit Parisien* in the vain hope that they might be able to glean some facts from reading between the lines. Even Nazi-sanctioned news was better than no news at all.

From Paris to Poland, the people lived on rumours which were known to be unreliable, but the passing on of what amounted to little more than gossip and wishes united a population denied access to information. As one French historian observed, it was a mixture of credulity and cynicism which offered hope that things would get better and, at the same time, satisfied the national penchant for pessimism.

And there was reason to be pessimistic. Rationing and shortages led to queues that were so long, gaps had to be left to allow pedestrians access to the pavement and Parisians had to allocate much of their day to standing in line. Journalist Jacques Biélinky queued for three hours in the first months of the occupation to buy potatoes and another five hours to buy sausages.

A noisy dissent

'The emphasis that is laid on the life of Paris during the period of military occupation is designed to show that French cultural life is flourishing as impressively as before the occupation,' said the *Observer* in September 1941, adding, 'the German authorities indirectly claim credit as the rebuilders of French cultural life'.

Radio, too, was mobilized by the Germans. They had exploited its potential from the earliest days of the dictatorship and believed that they could convince the French to accept the New Order by recruiting prominent French politicians to endorse their policies. The ministers of Marshal Pétain's Vichy government willingly disseminated Nazi propaganda vilifying the 'decadent' Allies, their 'jungle music' and their supposed Jewish-Masonic financiers, but the largely sceptical French preferred to tune in to the BBC, which broadcast French language programmes, the inspiring speeches of General de Gaulle and the Free French government in exile and, most important of all, the news. At 9.30 pm every evening, much of France came to a standstill to hear the BBC news in secret, with their ear right up to the radio. Having then satisfied their hunger for largely unbiased information, they returned to Radio Paris, with its mix of light frothy dance music, soap operas and interviews with ordinary Parisians recorded on the streets, returning to their own conversations and chores whenever the anti-Semitic rants resumed.

The French resented being forbidden from singing their national anthem *La Marseillaise*, which the Germans considered an act of resistance, but found other ways to express their abhorrence of their oppressors and the Vichy traitors. The lies of Vichy Propaganda Minister Philippe Henriot were ridiculed in a song that set new words to a popular tune.

In the cinemas, in the anonymity of the dark, they expressed their loathing for the Boche. An anonymous letter received in March 1941 by Radio Londres, the French service of the BBC, recorded the reaction to a newsreel of Hitler's meeting with Mussolini:

'Oh you should have heard the din! Everyone was whistling and shouting and stamping their feet, cursing these two old cronies with words that I dare not repeat.' The audience was warned to keep silent, but the next time the newsreel was screened 'the whole of the auditorium succumbed to a sudden and noisy cold! Everyone was coughing and sneezing!'

The problem became so endemic that on occasion, patrons were forced to provide doctors' certificates to prove that their chronic coughing was genuine.

Boos and abuse were so common that cinema managers were forced to keep the lights on while the newsreel was being shown in order to identify anyone expressing disrespect. Doors were locked so that none could leave or time their arrival to avoid the dreaded newsreel. By 1943, the customary reaction to Nazi propaganda in cinemas was silence.

Resistance

Those who were not persuaded to co-operate by Nazi propaganda, nor intimidated by the Nazis' threats, risked betrayal by their own countrymen, who might turn informer to curry favour with the enemy.

The French authorities had cracked down on their own communists following the signing of the German–Soviet pact in August 1939, so former members of the party were deemed to be enemies of the state. The only Frenchmen and women these politicians and city councillors could trust were members of the resistance, who now had to supply them with forged identity papers, provisions and supply coupons. These had to be stolen from town halls, preferably in the villages, where security was lax.

Marshal Pétain when he appeared in court in 1945 charged with sabotaging French democracy and collaborating with the Nazis. He was sentenced to death but this was commuted to life imprisonment because of his advanced age.

Knowing that the resistance were active in those areas, the Germans set up roadblocks and checkpoints outside many French towns and villages, but the maquis, the rural guerrilla bands, frequently recruited girls and young women to carry weapons and forged documents among the food, whom the Germans would let through in the belief that the girls were merely involved in the black market.

But the Germans were not the only ones to be feared. Every village seemed to have its 'Collabo' family who would inform on their neighbour in return for extra rations and other preferential treatment.

In Vichy, the atmosphere of fear and suspicion was all the more intense because it was effectively a fascist state run by Frenchmen, collaborators all. Resentment was compounded by the fact that Vichy had abolished the Republic which had promised 'Liberty, Equality and Fraternity' for all, regardless of race, creed or colour. In its place was Pétain's motto 'Work, Family and Fatherland', supporting an oppressive, reactionary regime policed by 35,000 *milice*, the French fascist militia recruited from the prisons, where they had been promised a pardon and payment in return for enforcing the law dictated by Berlin. The degree with which these men were hated and despised can be determined from the fact that 10,000 of them were summarily executed during the 'purge' immediately after liberation in 1944.

In the summer of 1943, Pétain's right-hand man, Pierre Laval, initiated the round-up of all able-bodied French men for compulsory labour service in Germany, which sent many scurrying for the hills to join the resistance, a year after Laval had organized the round-up of French Jews to ingratiate himself with his Nazi masters.

The sorrow and the pity

For some, their reason for joining the resistance was a simple matter of resentment at the restrictions imposed upon them by the invader and the outrage they felt at finding themselves second-class citizens in their own country. One such experience for resistance leader Émile Coulaudon, who took the name Colonel Gaspard in the Auvergne maquis, was the sight of Germans eating locally farmed beef steaks in a restaurant and being told that there were none for him and his friends. When the Germans imposed a curfew which effectively imprisoned the French in their own homes, Gaspard resolved to organize a campaign of armed resistance.

The primary aim of resistance, he told documentary maker Marcel Ophüls, was to create 'a climate of psychological fear', to undermine the Germans' belief that they were invincible and that they had intimidated the French population to the point where they were too afraid to rise up and strike back. The maquis knew they had no hope of inflicting a military defeat on the enemy, who were vastly superior in terms of numbers and arms – they could never kill enough Germans to make a difference as Gaspard put it – but they could slow them down, cut off their lines of communication, disrupt the transportation of men and material and harass German troops at every opportunity, in spite of reprisals.

The Germans came to think of the resistance fighters as 'terrorists' and 'bandits' because they would not play fair, as they saw it. They did not wear identifying armbands or uniforms and relied on 'dirty tricks'. One German officer stationed in France remembered an incident in which his platoon was ambushed by the resistance posing as agricultural workers tending their crops. As the German soldiers marched past, the 'workers' whipped out their concealed weapons and gunned down 14 Germans.

To the Germans, the massacre of unarmed civilian hostages seemed a perfectly reasonable response.

Waiting out the war

But while many risked capture and torture at the hands of the Gestapo and thereafter summary execution, others sought to remain inactive and impartial for as long as they could. This attitude incensed active members of the resistance such as Colonel Gaspard, who detested those who claimed that the only reason they did nothing was that they didn't know how to contact the resistance, or that they kept a revolver in a drawer to kill a German, but never had the opportunity to fire it. There were even those who shamelessly pretended to be members of the maquis so that they could loot from their own countrymen with impunity.

Former resistance leader Georges Bidault believes it was only a matter of temperament that determined who fought and who stood idly by and waited out the war: 'Some people are resisters by nature – naturally headstrong. Others, on the contrary, try to adapt to the circumstances and try to get what they can out of it.'

Emmanuel d'Astier de La Vigerie, founder of the Libération resistance movement, was convinced that the majority of those who joined the resistance were outsiders like himself, who could not have lived with the knowledge that they had failed to act when they had the opportunity to fight and therefore found a certain 'dignity' and self-respect in committing themselves to a noble and patriotic cause. But when he told his superiors in the defeated French army of his intention to join, they said he was 'mad' and asked why he didn't simply surrender as they were doing. They saw no purpose in prolonging a battle that was lost. In their eyes, anyone who joined the underground was denying reality.

To these men, it was to their country's lasting shame that the French government headed by Pétain was the only government of an occupied country to willingly and actively collaborate with the enemy.

The Dark Years

The French civil authorities were so anxious not to offend their German overseers that they frequently anticipated orders and, on occasion, even initiated their own restrictive practices to appease their masters. Many were revolted by the eagerness with which their French officials complied with Nazi edicts. Slowly but surely, people began to open their eyes and what they saw led them to change their minds regarding the nature of the occupation forces, who were no longer making an effort to appear affable or accommodating.

The round-ups of French workers to be sent to Germany as forced labour incensed the many people who had believed German assurances that they would be treated humanely and not as a conquered nation. And the deportation of Jews in cattle wagons woke others to the reality of Nazi ideology, even if the full extent of their genocide was not yet known.

But the single most alarming event of the so-called 'Dark Years' came on 11 November 1942, when the Wehrmacht crossed the demarcation line into unoccupied France under the pretext that they needed to defend the southern French coast against Allied invasion. The Allies had landed in North Africa three days before and the Germans feared a landing in the south of France was only weeks away.

Scarcity and survival

The one thing that dominated French people's lives for the next four years was food. The health of their children was paramount in the

Portrait of a French maquis, an unnamed resistance fighter, taken by Carl Mydans for Life *magazine, 1944.*

minds of many parents, who feared the return of diseases such as rickets caused by malnutrition.

But it wasn't only food and fuel that was rationed. Textiles, too, were scarce as they were no longer being imported from the colonies. When nylons became scarce, women took to painting their legs so that they would look as if they were wearing stockings.

Hunger and cold demoralized the greater part of the population, but as one former British agent remembers, French workers would share what little they had with someone who risked their life to bring liberation nearer. Denis Rake was an SOE operative who quickly learned that his best hope of survival lay with the farmers and railway workers, who would give their last piece of bread to keep him alive, while the 'better off' were reluctant, as they had more to lose if the Germans found out they were offering shelter to a British agent.

Refugees

Henriette Dodd was 12 years old and living with her widowed mother in Chauny, a small provincial town in northern France, when the Germans invaded in the spring of 1940.

Even before the 'Phoney War' (the uneasy period after war was declared before hostilities began) there were food shortages in the region and forged ration coupons appeared on the burgeoning black market.

When the first air raids came, the civilian population hurriedly organized an evacuation and took to the roads, leaving their possessions behind. Henriette was comparatively lucky in finding a train to take her, her mother and grandmother away from the fighting to the Massif Central, a mountainous region in the south of the country. In the village of Brive-la-Gaillarde they were allocated two rooms, which they shared with six other people in a large house, where their fear and uncertainty was exacerbated by the discomfort and lack of the most basic needs.

There was no bakery or butcher's shop in the vicinity and the one loaf of bread they had managed to find had to be rationed to last them a week. A butcher's van brought meat they would previously have refused to eat – brains, liver and kidneys which were fit only for animals (or the peculiar tastes of Parisians) – and milk had to be coaxed from the cow.

After France surrendered, the refugees were informed they had to return to their homes and so Henriette and her mother went back to Chauny, where they had run a small hotel. They found the Germans had occupied all but two of the rooms and that they had eaten all the provisions Madame Dodd and her daughter had hidden under the floorboards prior to their evacuation. But the occupation was 'bearable' because their 'lodgers' were highly disciplined and French civilians were able to take any complaints to the *Kommandantur* (the Commandant's Headquarters), where serious breaches of discipline would be punished by transfer to the Eastern Front.

Daily life under German occupation was demoralizing and fraught even after many had begrudgingly begun to accept it. In the early months of the war, the Germans were strafed by British fighters, which flew low and illuminated their targets by dropping flares. French civilians were frequently injured and their homes damaged. But even when the air raids stopped and life resumed a routine, the French were under constant strain for fear that they might be taken hostage by the Germans as a reprisal for attacks by the resistance. Members of their families could be taken to labour camps and factories in the Reich; among the victims of such a fate was the uncle of Henriette Dodd.

Rationing

In addition to the lack of electricity, heating, gas and hot water in the early months of the occupation, food rationing reinforced the siege mentality, so that everyone was constantly reminded that they were prisoners in their own country. While the Germans lived on the fat of the land, requisitioning the best accommodation, food and wine for themselves, the general population were forced to live on 1,200 calories a day, roughly half of the required amount for a healthy diet. Shop owners and farmers seen as being too generous were frequently punished by being closed down for a week or two or, in rare cases, permanently. The Germans justified such measures by declaring that the French also had to feed the occupiers and a share of the country's produce (a third in most cases) was needed to be shipped to Germany, so allowing the population more than their allotted share was effectively stealing from the Reich. Hoping to incite anti-British feeling, they attempted to blame the shortages on the British blockade, but few of the French were taken in by this.

Even basic foodstuffs became a luxury, with coffee being substituted by chicory, which not only tasted bitter but also acted as a laxative if not drunk in moderation. Milk and eggs were often replaced with the powdered variety, while swede, which was in plentiful supply, replaced almost every other vegetable. Also rationed were butter and cheese. For the food-loving French, this made a demoralizing situation intolerable. Oddly enough, two commodities widely and freely available were wine and tobacco, which young adolescents were allowed in compensation for the lack of chocolate and other childhood treats.

A shortage of sugar and salt reduced most meals to a bland, tasteless mush and people were driven to try cooking things they would never have eaten otherwise. Beet, kale, rhubarb and turnips became staple ingredients in lieu of other vegetables, but these had to be eaten in moderation too when it became known that their leaves contained oxalic acid, which is toxic to humans and can cause severe gastroenteritis.

Even fresh fruit, fish and vegetables joined the list of essential produce available only with the requisite ration coupons. Those who owned poultry, pigs and livestock fared better than most, while their less affluent neighbours bred rabbits for the table.

Fears grew for children's health and vitamin biscuits were introduced to compensate for the lack of adequate nutrition. According to French historian Henry Rousso, the incidence of heart disease was significantly reduced in the middle-aged, who benefitted from the reduction of fat in their diet, while the infant mortality rate rose and malnourishment became common among the young and the elderly. The bitter winters of the war years brought further misery to those for whom shortages of coal and gas and erratic electricity supplies meant little or no hot water and heating. Children frequently sat in classrooms in their coats or skipped school altogether.

Clothes and fabrics were also in short supply, so enterprising and resourceful mothers converted curtains and bedding into new outfits, dying them to disguise their origin, while shoes had to be resoled with thin strips of wood. Rationing did not end with liberation, but dragged on until 1949. The motto of the occupation was 'make do and mend', a mentality which stayed with many for the rest of their lives.

How the other half lived

If an impartial observer had been able to ask a cross-section of the French population how they fared under German occupation, they would undoubtedly have been given very different impressions. With a population of approximately 40 million divided by class, culture and personal circumstances, it is impossible to make generalizations regarding the attitude and experience of one nation under armed occupation, particularly given the regional variation whereby some of the population lived under Vichy and others under the Germans.

It has been argued that the poorer section of the population endured the privations more easily, simply because they were conditioned to make do with less. However, the more affluent could bribe both German and French officials, if not with hard currency then with valuables and heirlooms, though this at a time when food was more prized than possessions. Those who profited during the occupation were those who put patriotism and principles to one side for the duration, namely the collaborators and the black marketeers, though few of them would live to enjoy their privileges after the Germans deserted them in July 1944.

The majority of the French people could be said to have made their own accommodation with the regime, complying with those regulations they could not avoid and circumventing those they could. After all, these were not French laws they were ignoring. It was, one could argue, their patriotic duty to disregard the enemy's edicts under which they were forced to live. Consequently, few saw anything wrong in sourcing their needs from the grey market, which involved making trips to the country to stock up on provisions they couldn't buy in the towns and cities, although they were acutely aware that they would be searched on their return at the railway station. Necessity also encouraged the growth of the barter system, which saw individuals exchanging items they no longer required for those they could not afford or find elsewhere.

Food prices tripled during the four years of occupation, according to some sources, and it was estimated that the majority of a family's income was spent on food, whereas it had only been between a third to a half prior to the war.

A pastor's defiance

There were many individual acts of defiance to the Germans in France, one of which was the action initiated by the Protestant pastor of Le Chambon-sur-Lignon, to the south-west of Lyons.

In defiance of Nazi racial policy, Pastor André Trocmé and his wife, Magda, encouraged the villagers to hide Jews – particularly children – and other fugitives so that they could not be transported to the camps during the mass round-ups. Incredibly, Trocmé managed to convince the inhabitants of other villages in the region to risk their lives to give sanctuary to the Jews, with the result that several thousand survived the war.

A man of principle, Pastor Trocmé refused to lie to the Germans or to the French authorities. He admitted that he had organized their safekeeping, but he simply refused to disclose where they were hidden. Consequently, he was imprisoned for a time, but he lived to see the Germans driven out of France.

Vichy

Vichy was the unlikely choice of capital for the collaborationist government of Marshal Pétain, but a fitting one. In the spring of 1940, this small, quiet spa town in the Auvergne, four and a half hours from Paris by train, attracted genteel old ladies and retired military men who wanted to enjoy their remaining years sitting in street corner cafés and watching the world pass by. It offered wealthy convalescents a casino, a golf course and more than 300 hotels. Pétain and his cabinet would make themselves comfortable in the Hotel du Parc while his ministers convened in adjacent hotels like an elderly gentlemen's club. But they were only fooling themselves if they imagined that they exercised any real power. Their purpose was merely to rubber-stamp Nazi decrees, which meant abolishing the trade unions, making membership of the Communist Party and the Freemasons illegal, prohibiting women from the professions and depriving Jews of their citizenship.

The British foreign secretary, Anthony Eden, thought the 84-year-old 'hero of Verdun' practically 'senile' by this time, while a celebrated French novelist who had to ingratiate himself with the regime in order to have a book approved by Pétain's censors described both the cabinet and the town as a 'cardboard façade'.

Pétain's government was seen by the majority of the population as little more than a figurehead for the Nazi administration, which played the aged French politicians in Vichy off against the even more fiercely pro-fascist collaborators in Paris, men such as Jacques Doriot and Marcel Deat, creating a rivalry that was intended to keep Pétain's ministers on their toes.

But Vichy was regarded as the legitimate government of occupied France by the outside world. More than 40 states engaged in formal diplomatic relations with Vichy, including Russia and the United States, while Britain – which enjoyed a 'difficult' relationship with the Pétain administration – only turned away to recognize the Free French government of de Gaulle in 1944.

'Old man' Pétain

But the French themselves were ambivalent towards Vichy. They tended to make a distinction between the marshal and his ministers, heavily influenced by their location. Those in the 'forbidden zone' of occupied France considered Vichy irrelevant, as they came under the direct rule of the Germans in Belgium. But as historian Richard Vinen notes in *The Unfree French* (2007), 'Its popularity ebbed and flowed in complicated ways, the overall trend was downwards and disenchantment with the regime set in relatively early, certainly by the middle of 1941.'

Only the children remained staunchly loyal to 'the old man', who was portrayed as a kindly grandfather figure in their comics and for whom they sang patriotic songs praising his beneficence, sacrifice and sense of duty in place of the banned *La Marseillaise*. Pro-Pétain rallies were almost exclusively attended by children, whose presence was compulsory.

There was an atmosphere of suspicion and paranoia in the so-called 'free zone', which was just as oppressive as that felt in the occupied zone, where Gestapo informants seemed to be lurking in every shadow. This was particularly noted by teachers and professors, who were obliged to give speeches at the start of each academic year in praise of the marshal and his policies. Private diaries of those who dared to keep such things frequently recorded the real thoughts of those forced to give these speeches, their belief that the lecture halls were bugged and the ways in which they circumvented the requirements by, for example, conveniently 'forgetting' to include anti-British sentiments in their address.

On 11 October 1940, diarist Henri Drouot recorded:

> Chabot made the required speech, eulogy of Pétain, commen-tary on the programmes published by the Vichy government; work, moral rule, the fatherland (!). He had to seem warm enough to satisfy the ministry and skilful enough not to contradict the ideas of the majority of the professors, who are very hostile to the government of the Marshal.

French itself was banned in Alsace, where the inhabitants faced deportation if they dared to speak their own language. French children in the region were compelled to join the Hitler Youth and the young men conscripted into the German army.

The division of France was a shrewd move on behalf of the Nazis, who were at once relieved of the responsibility and the manpower required to administer two-fifths of the country that had been flooded with an estimated ten million refugees fleeing from their homes in the north. It also gave the Germans a free hand to plunder the resources and treasures of the occupied zone. During the exodus, 100,000 civilians had died, far more than were lost by the army in the Battle of France.

Wine – a bitter crop

The French wine producers of the Loire valley are a superstitious group. They have a saying that a poor crop is a bad omen and that an exceptionally poor crop is a sure sign that war is coming. The harvest of 1939 produced an uncommonly bad harvest; the following spring saw the Germans raiding the wine cellars and transporting what French premier Édouard Daladier called the Republic's 'crown jewels' back to Germany, just as the rustic prophets had predicted.

It was galling for the French, who valued their wines as highly as their art, so much so that on the eve of war, the government had sent the army to the Loire and surrounding countryside to save the grape harvest. They had also delayed conscription for vineyard workers to ensure that the year's crop was bottled before the hated Boche could savour it.

But it was all in vain. Bad weather saw that the last peacetime harvest was inferior and there was nothing that could be done to save it.

The fine restaurants of Paris and other French cities would have to sacrifice their vintage wines to satisfy their discerning patrons. There was nothing palatable from the great vineyards of 1939–40. Cask after cask was poured on to the ground and prayers offered for a swift victory, for it was said that the grapes would be sour until France was free again.

The Germans were unconcerned. They did not make a distinction between newly bottled wines and the practically priceless vintages that had been kept for decades in the dank cellars to mature. They simply rolled up at the gates to the Bordeaux, Burgundy and Vouvray vineyards and ordered the owners to empty their cellars on to the trucks that would take the precious bottles to Berlin, Berchtesgaden and Carinhall, Göring's

A sergeant distributes wine bottles to German soldiers upon a train, June 1940. The Germans robbed the French of as much wine as they could carry home.

private hunting lodge. The owners could do nothing but stand and watch as crates of Château Latour, Château Lafite Rothschild, Château Mouton Rothschild, Romanée-Conti and Château d'Yquem – names to delight a connoisseur – were loaded aboard. To the Germans this was simply part of the plunder, but for the old aristocratic families who cultivated the land and affixed their crest to every bottle, it was a heartbreaking sight. These crates represented their inheritance, an heirloom they had been entrusted to preserve. Now the 'old enemy' would be guzzling vintage champagne like cheap table wine.

The Phoney War

The French had one piece of luck during that last summer of peace: the period of eerie calm before the storm which they called 'the Phoney War', which they used to hide the most precious bottles where the enemy would never find them. A single vineyard concealed 100,000 bottles in limestone caves at Beaune in the Côte d'Or, a fraction of the stock smuggled out by the larger producers before the Germans arrived to clear out their cellars.

Restaurants, too, scrambled to save their stocks from the barbarians, as the French saw them. Parisian restaurateur André Terrail boasted a 400-page wine list, which had been accumulated over a lifetime, and was not going to allow Hitler's hordes to take it from him. His son Claude took emergency leave from the air force to save 10,000 bottles, which he and the staff of La Tour d'Argent, on the Quai de la Tournelle, hid in the walls for safekeeping until after the war.

The Wine führers

In total, an estimated two million bottles of vintage wine, champagne and cognac were seized by the Germans and transported back to the Reich.

After the initial looting spree, Göring sought to do business with the French wine producers, though he had no intention of paying the asking price. In his capacity as Reich Minister of Economic Policy for the occupied countries, he devalued the franc so that German soldiers would get more for their marks. French perfume, fashion and cosmetics were bought for a fraction of their true value and copious amounts of expensive champagne and cognac were consumed by those who couldn't taste the difference between Château Mouton Rothschild and cheap bistro plonk.

Göring considered France to be no more than a municipality of the Reich and determined to steal all he could, whereas Foreign Minister Von Ribbentrop, a former champagne salesman, tried in vain to convince him that Germany would gain more in the long term if it gave France a degree of sovereignty and offered to pay for those things it coveted.

To that end, Göring enlisted the expertise of German wine merchants who had been buying from the French for decades and who could exploit the good relationship with the owners of the more exclusive vineyards.

But when the German 'wine führers', as the locals called them, returned to France, they were not welcomed as they had been before the war. Their former friends knew they had little choice but to accept the price they were offered and, with the devalued franc, they were being forced to sell at a fraction of the market price.

They naturally resented this and the fact that the Germans would be selling it on at a considerable profit, but the only alternative was to pour their precious wine on to the ground. Some chose to do so rather than concede defeat.

But there was a mutual respect that even the war could not destroy. Heinz Bomers purchased inferior wines from a French vineyard, despite knowing he risked losing his official status and perhaps even his life by doing so. At another vineyard, he had an ordinary wine relabelled Château Mouton Rothschild and shipped off to Berlin.

The war years yielded an equally bitter crop that might have been saved had there not also been a sugar shortage, which could have been used to boost the alcohol content, and a shortage of eggs, which could have been added to reduce the clouding that occurred in poorly processed wine.

It was only when the Germans finally retreated from France back behind the Siegfried Line that the vineyards of the Loire valley produced a vintage crop.

Over the river

The neighbouring villages of Saint-Aignan and Noyers were separated by the river Cher, which ran along the demarcation line. This meant that Saint-Aignan, south of the river, was in the 'free zone' administered by Vichy, while Noyers in the north was in the occupied zone under the direct rule of the Germans.

Letters had to be smuggled from one side to the other by children as they were not searched as thoroughly as the adults.

The Gendarmerie

It is a sad and sobering fact that without the willing collaboration of the police in each occupied country, the Germans would not have been able to control the population as effectively as they did. By convincing the civil authorities of the need for an orderly transition to a military administration, the Germans were allocated tens of thousands of willing accomplices in the police, who found themselves in the unenviable position of having to restrain and subdue a population who had not broken any laws and who were not a threat to public order.

Many in the administration showed a willingness to co-operate and there are those who argue that the French police became a branch of the Gestapo in all but name. It was the Gendarmerie who actively participated in the round-ups and controlled the prisoners when they could have refused to co-operate. It has been said that the Gestapo would not have been as successful in terrorizing the population and identifying 'subversive' elements if the French police had not been so eager to assist them.

French political prisoners witnessed their comrades being brutalized and executed by French police, even when the Germans were not present. In many cases they initiated actions, which led directly to the murder of countless French civilians. In one of the most shameful episodes of the occupation, it was allegedly the French police who delivered 4,051 children for deportation to the Vélodrome d'Hiver stadium in Paris on 16 and 17 July 1942, when the Germans had only instructed them to round up those over the age of 16. The enthusiasm with which the French police carried out their task earned the praise of their German masters, as did Vichy Prime Minister Pierre Laval, who ordered that the children be separated from their parents and sent to a different concentration camp, despite having it in his power to rescind the order to transport them. For his role in this shameful affair, Laval was executed after the war.

It is an uncomfortable fact that in both Vichy France and the occupied north, the police did more than simply obey orders issued by their superiors at the behest of the Germans. The extent to which the Gendarmerie willingly and even enthusiastically collaborated with the Nazis has only recently come to light, as previously the true figures were obscured by the insidious practice of discounting those who had been stripped of French citizenship. This applied mainly but not exclusively to the Jews, who it was claimed had not suffered such numerical losses as in other occupied countries, but – it turned out – because only those Jews who still retained their French citizenship had been included in the statistics.

Apologists for the Vichy regime have falsely claimed that more French Jews survived than those of any other occupied country, but they exclude the tens of thousands who were stripped of their citizenship in order to manipulate the figures. France delivered the same number of Jews to the Nazi death camps as all the other countries under German control.

The myth has persisted that only a few 'black sheep' among the police turned traitor and that the majority of the force remained passive during the occupation, a damning indictment in itself and, as it transpires, a false one. As contemporary police reports, periodical reports by the Prefect of Police and the police inspectorate (Inspection Générale des Services Administratifs) reveal, far too many were active and willing participants in the round-up, interrogation and execution of French citizens, including Algerians, Armenians and other immigrant resistance fighters.

The Milice

With the French police acting as an instrument of the occupation, the Germans were able to reduce the number of their forces in the 'free zone' to the south of the demarcation line and deploy them elsewhere. If they had not been able to rely on the French police to enforce German military decrees and to do their dirty work for them, as Simon Kitson puts it in 'From Enthusiasm To Disenchantment: The French Police and the Vichy Regime, 1940–44', they might have been overstretched on another front and the resistance might have proven more effective.

By 1943, Vichy had established the Milice, an extreme right-wing paramilitary militia to rival the regular police, a strategy historian Simon Kitson observes is common to many dictatorships in order to hold on to power by adopting the policy of divide and rule. But the police rank and file were ideologically aligned with Vichy as they shared a common enemy, the communists, who had vilified the police in their pamphlets and newspapers in the interwar years. It was therefore not surprising that the police willingly handed over suspected communists to the Germans and didn't enquire as to what became of them.

The same can be said of the Jews, who conveniently fell into a second category – immigrants – which both the police and the Pétain government viewed with deep suspicion. Of the 76,000 Jews deported during the Vichy years, many of whom perished in the death camps, the vast majority were rounded up by the French police, who saw them primarily as 'foreigners' and therefore legitimate targets.

As early as the summer of 1942, support for Vichy was in decline and the police were demoralized. None of the promised rewards had materialized, criminality had increased significantly, particularly among the young, and police were being asked to do what they considered degrading duties, such as arresting women who had paid for illegal abortions. Instead of becoming an elite unit, they were overworked and under-resourced. They were told there was no money for new uniforms, that shifts would have to be increased and that in some towns, there were simply too few men to patrol effectively. It was not uncommon to find that Allied bombing had forced the police to use shops and even local bars as makeshift offices or to neglect to fill out reports because they couldn't afford to buy a new typewriter. More crucially, those who were armed rarely had enough ammunition.

By the following spring, there was a climate of mutiny in Marseille, prompting the prefect to request the transfer of his entire force of 5,000 men to another district because he could not rely on their loyalty.

Predictably, many began to question their role and drifted away to the resistance. For some their motivation was patriotism or compassion for the victims, but for others it was shame. They felt the need to atone for their participation in past *Aktions*, as the Germans called their round-ups, or that they had discredited the uniform by their association with the Nazis. Others feared being denounced to the resistance, who assassinated officers they believed had betrayed them.

More than 1,000 members of the Gendarmerie were arrested and subsequently deported as political prisoners and the German police identified one in ten members of the Combat resistance group as former members of the French police force.

As Kitson points out, by 1943, the police had lost any respect they might have had for the Vichy regime and their superiors who supported it. By introducing a forced labour scheme for all French men between the ages of 20 and 22, Pétain's puppet government had lost its authority, both with their own people and the Germans.

The latter were forced to become more active in matters of law and order, to endorse the Milice as the official arm of the occupation or risk losing control, a move they knew would be resented by the population.

The police force became a refuge for those seeking to avoid the forced labour programme and therefore a body sympathetic to the resistance. Gradually, they became less diligent and reliable in carrying out orders they saw as contrary to the spirit of the Republic, although certain groups composed mainly of anti-communists, such as the Groupes Mobiles de Réserve in Marseilles and the Brigades Spéciales in Paris, continued to hound the resistance until the liberation.

By the summer of 1944, it was simply too late for them to change sides and nothing they might have done could atone for the crimes they had committed during the Vichy years. Besides, many were die-hard fascists, who fervently believed the resistance was the enemy within and a covert arm of the Soviet Union.

Zazous

It could be argued that the Zazous, a French jazz-crazy youth cult of the occupation who dressed like their cool counterparts in the USA, were not sticking two fingers up at their Nazi oppressors, but at the regressive, grey-haired ultra-conservatives in the Vichy regime.

Pétain and his ageing ministers symbolized the old guard, whom the youth of France would have rebelled against whether the Germans were occupying the country or not. But the fact that Vichy was actively collaborating with the Nazis gave the Zazous a certain cachet. To flaunt long hair in France during the occupation was more than a declaration of independence; it was an act of protest in itself. It defied the Vichy government's decree of 27 March 1942, which required barbers to collect cut hair to make slippers and jumpers.

The Pétain regime disapproved of the nation's youth, whom they condemned as immoral and workshy. The young men and women of the Zazous were equally contemptuous of their collaborationist leaders.

In identifying with black American musicians and adopting what they imagined were their mannerisms, their clothing and their music, the Zazous were also expressing the rejection of their own culture which, as one observer expressed, was 'tarnished by complicity'.

Swing!

The Zazous had their own particular way of thumbing their noses at authority: a tribal dance to be performed in front of public buildings that had been commandeered by the Germans or the Vichy officials. They would hop on the spot, touch their hips three times and scream 'Swing!' then shrug their shoulders twice and turn their heads to one side.

Even when they were standing still, lounging in a suitably louche manner, it was easy to identify a member of the Zazous (who took their moniker from a Cab Calloway hit). They were almost all in their late teens and evidently had the money and leisure to dress fashionably and hang around cafés and clubs doing nothing much at all but 'digging' the music and eyeballing the coolest kids in town. They were inheritors of a steaming jazz scene that had established itself in Paris and Marseilles during the interwar years, when some of the hottest names in American popular music had migrated to France, where the colour of their skin was rarely commented upon and the music they made was embraced by people of all ethnicities.

By 1942, the movement had caught the attention of the French press, especially the collaborationist papers, who condemned it as unpatriotic, while the German administration generally considered it harmless and of little interest to them. One French jazz musician, Johnny Hess, namechecked the Zazous in his 1942 hit, *Je suis swing*.

Je suis swing

The male members of the Zazous wore wide, knee-length jackets and baggy trousers (commonly known as zoot suits) with garishly coloured socks and carried umbrellas even on cloudless days. Many also sported a neat moustache, but it was the flamboyant suits which irritated their elders, as this was a time of austerity, conformity and fabric rationing. If the old guard grew hot under the collar at the sight of the boys, they became positively apoplectic when they saw the girls, who wore provocatively short skirts, wide-shouldered jackets and had their hair coiffured Hollywood-style. They were the personification of movie star chic, while their young men aped the cool laid-back attitude of their idols such as Cab Calloway, Count Basie, Billy Eckstine and Duke Ellington.

French designer Christian Dior found it repellent, but then it was intended as a political and personal statement and not a fashion statement. In his words, 'Hats were far too large, skirts far too short, jackets far too long, shoes far too heavy... For lack of other materials, feathers and veils, promoted to the dignity of flags, floated through Paris like revolutionary banners.'

The Zazous and the Jews

Being so visible meant the Zazous were easy to find and many were rounded up and beaten by the Vichy thugs of the Jeunesse Populaire Française, a fascist youth organization, who resented their freedom, wealth and leisure. The fascists took a perverse delight in shearing their victims' hair and running through the streets screaming 'Scalp the Zazous'.

They were also condemned by the collaborationist newspaper *La Gerbe* on 25 June 1942, while another pro-Nazi paper published offensive cartoons depicting young French jazz lovers as the unwitting victims of avaricious Jews and their Bolshevik friends:

> We are having great difficulty in eliminating the venom of Americanism. It has entered our customs, impregnated our civilization. We must devote our utmost efforts against these transgressions of taste and bearing: the decline of critical faculties, the follies of n****r jazz and swing, the contagion of our youth by American cocktail parties.

They may have been tolerated by the Germans, who were bemused more than offended, but in June 1942, the Zazous took the courageous step of showing solidarity with the Jews, who were ordered to identify themselves by wearing a yellow star on their clothes in public. The Zazous took to wearing yellow stars, too, but with 'Swing', 'Zazou' or 'Goy' emblazoned on them, in the place of '*Juif*' (for males) or '*Juive*' (for females).

That summer, French officials mounted raids on known Zazous clubs and cafés and sent the offenders to work camps in the countryside, as if they were addicts in need of isolation. There, the nonconformists were humiliated, bullied and brutalized. They had their hair cut, were forced to wear drab uniforms and were given menial, demeaning chores to do by representatives of Vichy's Ministry of Youth, which had been established in July 1940 to oversee the moral welfare, education and productivity of the nation's youth. In short, they conditioned and indoctrinated the young people of France to act without thinking and to think only along prescribed lines endorsed by their pro-fascist leaders.

Sadly, this appeared to have the desired effect because from that year on, the remaining members of the Zazous went underground. Eventually the fashion disappeared from the jazz clubs, cafés and cellars along the Champs Élysées, Montmartre and the Latin Quarter and their raucous, life-affirming beat fell silent.

The resourceful French

Wartime restrictions were suffered by many and overcome by others.

With petrol rationed and travel restricted, the French devised the taxi bicycle, which added a large hanging box to a bike (more often a tandem), fitted with canvas to protect the passengers from the wind and rain.

With tobacco in short supply, other natural ingredients were tried with varying degrees of success. A Monsieur Alexandre discovered that chopped nettles and chestnut leaves gave a satisfying smoke, though the aroma was extremely unpleasant. The 26-year-old unemployed insurance worker sold more than 150,000 packs of 'Eco-Tabac' at 2.80 francs a pack, which gave him an enviable income. But his success was short-lived. He was arrested and sentenced in December 1941 by the Chambre Correctionnelle de la Seine for selling cigarettes without paying the required tobacco tax.

Another enterprising Parisian published the following advert in the *Gazette du Palais*: 'Smokers, forget the lack of tobacco: you will never be short of REXOL cigars and cigarettes. Free information and samples on request.' Rexol were pseudo-medical wooden cigarettes, prescribed to protect delicate throats. Normally sold for between six and ten francs, the enterprising advertiser asked for 38.45 francs to ship them to his customers, which gave him a very healthy profit of about 24 francs per order. He was sentenced to four months' imprisonment on 2 February 1942 for profiting from the black market.

With oil and paraffin difficult to procure and gas supplies erratic, the French devised other means of keeping warm in the colder months. Those without work spent hours in post offices, banks and libraries and were tolerated by the staff, who generally sympathized with their plight. The Bordeaux Municipal Library saw the number of 'readers' rise from a pre-war figure of 44,336 in 1939 to 60,346 in 1940. Figures stayed elevated throughout the war years.

Newspapers advised readers not to throw away their papers but to use them to stuff their shoes and line their jackets and coats in cold weather. But the most ingenious invention was the fireless cooker, which required no power to heat it. Food only had to be warmed in a pan of boiling water before being transferred to the box filled with straw, cushions or crumpled paper. The straw retained the heat and the food continued to cook in its own warmth. It took three times as long to cook through, but it made it possible to cook without gas or electricity. The technique had been used by campers and agricultural workers since the early 19th century, but the war made it popular again. The Zazous would not let wartime restrictions cramp their style, so when hair oil was hard to find they used salad oil instead to make their hair shine.

During the occupation, even the most commonplace items became scarce. Instead of glue, garlic was used which meant that school art classes were restricted to warm days when the windows could be left open.

The black market

The scarcity of fresh produce was exacerbated by the fact that many farmers had been killed during the fighting, either in the crossfire between the French, BEF (British Expeditionary Force) and the Germans, in artillery barrages or as a consequence of the bombing and strafing of fleeing refugees by German fighters. In Vichy, the administration ordered that abandoned lands must be cultivated, particularly in the large Sologne and Crau region. Workers were encouraged to maintain allotments and were provided with tools, seeds and practical help. Even the famous Jardin des Tuileries was given over to growing vegetables, to the dismay of many Parisians.

With fresh meat impossible to obtain, some had taken to killing and eating cats. The practice was so prevalent by October 1941 that several French newspapers published warnings that they were running great risks of contracting a fatal infection as cats could be carrying a bacillus from eating rats. Whether the warnings had any effect is not known, but about the same time market traders in Lyons were selling ravens for ten francs apiece and the number of pigeons roosting in Bordeaux's Pierre Laffitte Square drastically decreased from 5,000 to 89 (though it is not known how they could be so certain of these figures). In Brive, a partridge was auctioned for 1,650 francs, more than an unskilled labourer earned in a month.

In such dire times, the Church refused to condemn the black marketeers and on 13 December 1941 in the *Semaine Religieuse de Paris*, Cardinal-Archbishop of Paris Monseigneur Suhard publicly absolved all those who obtained 'the necessities of existence' by these 'modest extra-legal operations'.

But the problem was not those who felt they had little choice but to pay black market prices, but rather those who exploited them. Typically, the average item cost double on the black market. One kilogram of Gruyère cheese, for example, cost 21 francs before the war but 50 francs on the black market, while parmigiano would have been 40 francs a kilo before the war, but was 70 francs on the black market.

BRITAIN AND THE CHANNEL ISLANDS – 30 June 1940
Between a rock and a hard place

For the inhabitants of Guernsey and Jersey, it was an agonizing time. The spring of 1940 saw the Channel Islands cut off from the mainland and the population effectively imprisoned within 200 miles of the English coast. The majority of their young men had left that winter to join the British army, although they were not subject to conscription. Thousands of children had been evacuated to England, Scotland or Wales, accompanied by teachers and parents. However, 4,500 school-aged children remained on Jersey to continue life as usual. Just 1,000 remained on Guernsey, including those from one school that had intended to leave but missed their boat. A lack of planning by the British authorities in London led to conflicting instructions, misunderstandings and confusion.

British troops had departed without warning on 15 June, having determined that their positions were too vulnerable to attack, but they deliberately kept their departure secret from the civilians to avoid panic. The lieutenant governors of both islands, official representatives of the British government, sailed at the same time, leaving the civil administration to cope as best they could and the community feeling it had been abandoned to its fate and condemning the lieutenant governors' departure as a betrayal.

The remaining population could only watch the dogfights overhead between the vastly outnumbered RAF and Göring's Luftwaffe with increasing anxiety, for if the Luftwaffe ruled the skies over the Channel, Britain would be invaded that summer and all hope of liberation would die.

Only weeks before, the tourist office had been promoting the islands as idyllic holiday resorts, but occupation by the Germans was now imminent. On 28 June, the Luftwaffe bombed the harbours and Guernsey's main town, St Peter Port, inflicting minor damage and killing 34 civilians.

No military value

The arrival of German troops on 30 June was a bitter blow for British morale, which was already desperately low following the fall of France and the trauma of Dunkirk and became lower still when it was learnt that a single platoon had taken Guernsey without a shot being fired, for there were no troops left to defend it. Two weeks later, on 14 July, the main German force arrived by ship, evidently in no hurry to add the islands to the Reich.

Among the first acts imposed by the conquerors was a declaration stating that all civilians were now subject to German law and that the island would operate as if it was part of the continent. Clocks would be adjusted to continental time and all vehicles would have to drive on the right side of the road.

British currency was no longer legal. Instead, freshly printed vouchers or scrip would be circulated to pay for goods and services. The reaction of the islanders to being paid in valueless 'Monopoly' money can easily be imagined.

Guernsey and Jersey together with their satellite islands, Sark and Alderney, were the only part of the British Isles to be invaded and though the islands were not important strategically, their loss was keenly felt.

A Nazi marching band comes around the corner on Guernsey in 1940 in what looks like a scene from the film It Happened Here *(1964), which envisaged what would have happened if Britain had been invaded in 1940.*

That said, airfields on both Guernsey and Jersey had been used to launch bombing raids on Italian industrial targets the day after Italy joined the war against the Allies on 10 June. But still the islands were of no military value other than to provide the Germans with an outpost off the Normandy coast.

Impossible resistance

Of the 91,000 islanders, 66,000 remained; just over 24,000 in Guernsey, 41,000 in Jersey and fewer than 500 in Sark.

Alderney had been abandoned by all but a handful of inhabitants in expectation of the invasion and would become the site of the only concentration camps to be constructed on British soil. Approximately 6,000 forced labourers (many of them Russian prisoners and veterans of the Spanish civil war) were housed in the four camps, 600 of whom would die from malnutrition, cold and ill-treatment. They were immediately put to work laying mines and building fortifications.

The size of the islands, the lack of cover and the isolation meant that organized resistance was impossible, so the islanders could do little but suffer in silence and hope that one day the Allies would land in France and the Germans would accept defeat and surrender.

But this did not prevent some from making a desperate and ultimately futile cry for help. A poster now on display in the German Occupation Museum on Guernsey, dated 3 August 1941, is a chilling reminder of how merciless the Nazis could be:

> NOTICE. Louis Berrier, a resident of Ernes, is charged with having released a pigeon with a message for England. He was therefore sentenced to DEATH for espionage by the Court Martial and SHOT on second of August.

A question of guilt

The German occupation of the Channel Islands is a highly emotive subject for the islanders and is still capable of opening old wounds.

When the actor John Nettles, who had played fictional Jersey detective 'Bergerac' on TV in the 1980s, decided to write a book on the period, he encountered intense hostility from friends on the island as a result of his exposé: 'Either I don't tell this story and keep my friends,' he told the *Daily Express*, 'or I tell it and lose them all.'

Nettles, a former history graduate, was thorough and meticulous in his research, which uncovered a very different picture of life under the Nazis than the official version which has persisted to this day.

It is a 'myth', he says, that the occupation was a 'rather gentle, even benign affair'.

The enduring image of the period is of the disciplined invaders adhering to the Geneva Convention and making life 'uncomfortable but not horrendous' for the islanders, 'Unpleasant but not unendurable.' Nettles asserts that it was more complex than that: 'It is the story of a sustained attack on human values, of great suffering, venality and violence.'

Nettles regards the island leaders as 'naïve' in seeking to accommodate the Germans in the belief that they might be persuaded to be more lenient. He cites a bizarre incident which saw the Dame of Sark, Sybil Hathaway, invite German officers to a lobster dinner, an example of fraternization frowned upon by the British government after the war.

Guernsey bailiff Victor Carey was also investigated after the war and was deemed to be 'so mired in controversy' that the British 'didn't know whether to hang him or knight him'.

It could be argued that the officials were under pressure and had no choice but to co-operate with the Germans' demands, to instruct the population not to resist. Though their willingness to provide the Germans with lists of all the islands' inhabitants begs the question, when does co-operation become collaboration? Indeed, those lists were used by the Germans to deport thousands of 'undesirables' to concentration camps, many of whom were murdered, worked to death or died of ill-treatment, malnutrition or disease.

The officials who supplied the lists and those islanders who facilitated the transportation of the victims have always claimed that they had no knowledge of the Nazis' intentions, but it is that 'lack of awareness' which Nettles identifies as the silent and shameful crime the islanders refuse to acknowledge.

'The people are deeply, deeply hurt by the accusations that they are anti-Semitic,' he says, 'or that they were too much inclined to load the Jews on to the transporters... [but] they were there to be killed and they were deserving, therefore, of the protection of the civil authorities.'

Equally unwelcome are the reminders of just how willing some of the young women on the islands were to comfort the invaders. These so-called 'Jerrybags' were guilty of '*collaboration horizontale*', sleeping with the enemy. Others informed on their more courageous neighbours, leading in some cases to their deaths. Harold Le Druillenec and his sister Louisa Gould were sent to a concentration camp for harbouring an escaped Russian slave worker after a neighbour denounced them. Louisa died in the notorious Ravensbrück extermination camp, while her brother survived Bergen-Belsen.

Others were more fortunate. Albert Bedane offered shelter to three Russians and a Jewish woman, all of whom survived the occupation.

Resentment on both sides

There appears to have been a deliberate effort by many of the German officers to distance themselves from their Nazi leaders, to be seen instead as conscripted soldiers in uniform who would have preferred to be back home with their families, rather than as fanatical National Socialists. They were keen to demonstrate that peaceful coexistence was possible and to downplay the anti-German sentiment in the British press by running the Channel Islands as a 'model occupation', to borrow a phrase used by the Guernsey Attorney General, Ambrose Sherwill. They even allowed the islanders to trade freely with France, but there were restrictions on their movements, speech and any form of protest – even the painting of 'V for Victory' symbols on walls was severely punished. The possession of a radio set was forbidden and any adverse comments or other signs of disrespect during the screening of German newsreels were frowned upon with the threat to close the cinemas, which were some of the few outlets for entertainment available on the islands.

But the conciliatory approach was fatally undermined early on, when two Guernsey youths who had enlisted in the British army returned to conduct a reconnaissance mission. The Germans found out about them and promised to imprison them as POWs if they gave themselves up, but the moderate German officer who had given that assurance was overruled and when the young men surrendered, they were sentenced to be shot. The father of one of them committed suicide in despair and the death sentences were eventually commuted, but relations between the islanders and the occupation forces were irreparably damaged.

Sadly and perhaps inevitably, when those who had left for the mainland in June 1940 returned home, they encountered resentment from those who had stayed. Each side distrusted the other. Those who had left felt that they had been fighting the real war, while those who remained had not seen any of the fighting or suffered from the air raids. Many of those who had stayed felt that the others had deserted them in a time of need and were unable to convince them how hard it had been to live under the Nazis' tyranny, especially towards the end when food was so scarce many were reduced to a level of starvation.

What if? – The plan for Britain's occupation

If the Luftwaffe had won the Battle of Britain in September 1940 and Hitler had launched Operation Sea Lion, the invasion of Britain, what would life have been like for the British under Nazi occupation?

On 16 July 1940, after the shock defeat of the French, Dutch and Belgian armies, Hitler issued Directive 16, instructing his commanders to prepare for the invasion of the British Isles by air and sea: 'The aim of this operation will be to eliminate the English homeland as a base for the prosecution of the war against Germany. If necessary, to occupy it completely.'

These detailed plans survived the fall of the Nazi state and make sober reading more than 80 years later.

While the British licked their wounds after their shock defeat in France and waited for the inevitable onslaught, the German High Command spent six leisurely weeks drawing up detailed plans for the invasion and its aftermath. These documents reveal the Nazis intended a charm offensive to win over the civilian population while purging Britain's ruling elite and its dissident elements – namely the intellectuals, communists and Jews.

Ten thousand paratroopers were assigned for the initial attack on the south coast of England. Some 80,000 regular Wehrmacht troops and 4,000 tanks were to follow, crossing the Channel at its narrowest point on a wide front between Dover and Southampton. The attack would come in three waves, supported by a sky black with German bombers and their fighter escorts.

London was targeted for a devastating series of air raids that would have left it little more than rubble, just like Warsaw and Rotterdam.

'The Guide for Troops in Occupied England'

It was expected that within weeks victorious German troops would be marching down Whitehall, the weary and demoralized British army having been routed after their retreat from Dunkirk.

Britain was to be governed by Field Marshal Walther von Brauchitsch, the commander-in-chief of the German army as a reward for his part in the fall of France. Earlier that summer, he had issued a directive to the army ('*The Guide for Troops in Occupied England*') instructing them to take a 'firm and cautious attitude toward the civilian population'. It was initially issued to the troops who landed in the Channel Islands and von Brauchitsch expected his men to behave in a like manner on the mainland when the fighting was over. They were to be polite and to pay for everything they took from shops and businesses. Looting would be punished by death, as would acts of violence against unarmed civilians.

It was hoped that resistance would crumble if the Germans showed restraint and respect for their defeated enemy and that any incidents of armed resistance could be crushed before the main body of the invasion force had to be redeployed for the coming attack on Russia.

British POWs

Around two million British troops were expected to have surrendered during the invasion and these POWs were to be deported to prison camps on the continent, to ensure they could not be freed to fight again. They were to be held as hostages to discourage acts of sabotage and other acts of defiance, just as the French POWs had been following the fall of France. Once the Wehrmacht had secured the island, it was to have been policed by one of Reinhard Heydrich's many brutal underlings, SS-Brigadeführer Dr Franz Six. It would have been his task to arrest Britain's elite using a list of 2,800 names drawn up by the SS foreign intelligence agency. These included politicians (Churchill's Cabinet), members of the intelligentsia (including philosopher Bertrand Russell and novelist H.G. Wells), leading financiers and even prominent entertainers, such as Noel Coward, who were deemed to have 'insulted' the Nazis or whose sexuality was deemed to be 'deviant'. German emigrés such as Sigmund Freud were also named, as the Nazis intended to punish those who had turned their backs on the Fatherland and spoken out against the regime.

Dr Six was also to have headed six *Einsatzgruppen* death squads, who would have operated from Britain's major cities. Heydrich entrusted them with eliminating anti-Nazi elements:

'Your task is to combat all anti-German organizations, institutions and opposition groups.' And he specified the targets: Freemasons, Liberals, Marxists, politicized Church groups and the Jews.

Takeover of British institutions

The Nazis had compiled a directory of British institutions and political factions that might prove sympathetic and co-operative, in much the same way as the pro-Nazi factions in France and Denmark had been. If the Nazis secured their co-operation, they could delegate control of the population to this compliant civil administration and also hold them responsible for any acts of resistance. Among the likely quislings was Oswald Mosley, leader of the British Union of Fascists, as he was well-placed to influence pro-Hitlerites in the aristocracy, though the Nazis tended to favour established politicians who would have influence over the civil servants and could therefore be relied upon to see their policies put into practice.

There was also talk in Hitler's inner circle of enticing the discredited Duke of Windsor (formerly King Edward VIII) to return to Buckingham Palace to serve as prince regent and that a purse of 50 million Reichsmarks had allegedly been allocated to lure him back to Britain.

As in the Channel Islands, the British police would have come under the control of the SD (*Sicherheitsdienst*, or Security Force) and persuaded that it was in the interests of the country for them to continue to enforce law and order.

Subversive elements in Britain's universities and public schools were to have been dismissed, trade unions would have been banned and the Jews rounded up and sent to their deaths.

But the war might have taken a very different turn had the Germans occupied Britain. The British would not have been able to launch the second front in the Balkans that had forced Hitler to delay his attack on Russia by a crucial six weeks, just enough time for the German army to find itself bogged down outside Moscow when the Russian winter set in. And if Germany had managed to conquer the Soviet Union, it might have left Nazi-occupied Europe facing off against America, possibly with nuclear weapons deciding the fate of the world.

CHAPTER 4
UNDER THE JACKBOOT

The Nazi middlemen

The Nazis knew that, while they could subdue the population of the occupied territories using force, terror and intimidation, the business of governing the countries would be impossible without the co-operation of the civil authorities. In Western Europe, this would mean appointing the local mayor to act as a mediator between the military administration and the civilian inhabitants.

The majority of these officials were either elected or appointed to represent the will of the local inhabitants, but when the German administration assumed control, the individuals found themselves no more than a mouthpiece for the occupation forces. Seen by some as no better than collaborators and by others as hostages to the Nazis, they were in the unenviable position of being held personally responsible for all acts of resistance and civil disobedience. They would frequently be ordered to select those to be shot in retaliation for acts of terror and sabotage, as well as those who were to be taken hostage and executed in place of any resistance fighters who did not surrender themselves after committing an act against the occupation forces.

In rural areas, the mayors were often farmers with little formal education or experience outside of their community, whereas in the larger towns and cities they were more likely to be career politicians. All were faced with moral dilemmas on an almost daily basis, which were compounded by the confused and contradictory nature of Nazi bureaucracy.

Conflicting interests

The Nazi state was a chaotic structure comprising conflicting agencies and departments, each competing for the Führer's favours. It was a deliberate move on behalf of the Führer, who derived a childlike glee from causing confusion and whose cavalier attitude to the business of government led him to duplicate duties, so that his ministers and officials would be too busy arguing among themselves to pose a threat to his leadership. Ministers who were clearly incapable or incompetent were appointed well beyond their capabilities, knowledge or experience, partly to gratify Hitler's perverse sense of humour. He enjoyed watching others in discomfort. It amused him.

For example, Joachim von Ribbentrop, Hitler's foreign minister and a former champagne salesman, had a lamentable grasp of foreign affairs, while Robert Ley, head of the Labour Front, was afflicted with a speech defect. The latter amused Hitler, who took a sadistic delight in giving Ley as many public speaking engagements as he could find.

The Nazi state was a manifestation of its leader's irrational personality. He simply had no interest in governing. He was, by nature, an indolent daydreamer, who saw himself as a latter-day Caesar ruling by the force of his personality and guided by his visions and intuition. Politics had no appeal for him other than as a means of exercising power. He surrounded himself with sycophants and was too distrustful to delegate authority. As his press secretary observed, 'Instead of drawing to himself men of high character, rich experience and breadth of vision, he gave such persons a wide berth and made sure they had no chance to influence him... [He] permitted no other gods beside himself.'

Contradictions in government

It was this inconsistency and vagueness that led to a conflict of interests and contradictory policies when it came to governing the occupied countries. Matters were exacerbated by the directive many had received prior to the occupation from their superiors, which demanded them to co-operate with the enemy provided that their edicts did not conflict with national laws. Public officials were charged with the protection of the population and the discouragement and condemnation of all acts of resistance. Resistance was thought to be the work of communist agitators who were to be considered the enemy of the people since their

The Duke of Windsor visits a stock factory, 11 October 1937. To his right is Robert Ley, whom Hitler liked to mock for his speech defect.

acts were designed to disrupt the uneasy peace as much as the enemy's lines of communications and supplies. Nevertheless, many mayors took it upon themselves to assist downed Allied pilots with contacting the underground and with reaching a neutral country.

Matters were not helped by the fact that some of the occupied countries were without their guiding authority, the heads of state having fled into exile, leaving the mayors and other officials with little option but to co-operate with the Germans. Other countries, such as Belgium, retained their king and so the elected officials could claim that in co-operating with the Germans they were merely carrying out the will of their sovereign.

In Vichy France, the choice had been made for them. As elected or appointed officials, they were obliged to adhere to the pro-German policies endorsed by Pétain's puppet government.

As Nico Wouters notes in *Mayoral Collaboration under Nazi Occupation in Belgium, the Netherlands and France* (2016), the SS and its security services 'caused bureaucratic conflicts and intrigues that local functionaries could sometimes exploit'.

In both Holland and Belgium, for example, civil servants had been allowed to form informal cabinets which only made decision-making and implementation more difficult.

In Holland, local and regional politics varied by religion and political leaning, with some mayors being Protestant, others Catholic, some socialists and others installed by their Nazi sponsors. Naturally, this influenced the degree to which German laws and decrees were implemented or circumvented in the Netherlands.

In Belgium, the Flemish political parties were left unmolested in the belief that they would promote the idea of a Flemish state aligned with Germany, while the French-speaking Walloons appear to have been pro-German, to the extent that they supported their own pro-Nazi party, Rex, which actively collaborated with the occupation.

Day-to-day disorganization

The military conquest of Western Europe was comparatively easy in contrast with the day-to-day business of occupation. The population were in shock and uncertain of how they would be treated even if they complied with the curfews and restrictions, while armed resistance was sporadic and disorganized at first. What the population were not aware of was that the occupation forces were sharply divided between the High Command and the National Socialists as to how to administer the newly acquired territories.

In November 1939, Hitler had been forced to make a crucial concession to the Wehrmacht, namely to exclude party officials from the daily business of running the occupied countries. The army was assured that it would form a military administration. However, Hitler rarely kept his promises and as soon as the army chiefs had left the conference room, Himmler reminded the Führer of the necessity of allocating a role to his SS elite and to the Gestapo, the plain-clothes secret police to which Himmler had been appointed chief in 1934. The Reichsführer-SS knew that Hitler was suspicious of the Prussian officer elite, whom he thought overcautious and lacking in National Socialist ardour. Hitler believed, with reason, that the High Command looked down on him as 'the Bohemian corporal', the uneducated upstart who gambled recklessly with his forces on wild hunches and consulted astrological charts rather than military manuals when planning an attack. It was only a matter of time, they said, before his luck would run out.

Whenever Hitler was faced with a choice, he invariably solved it by giving in to both opposing parties and this is why the military administration remained in conflict with National Socialist agencies during the five years of the occupation.

The military administrations in Norway, Holland, Belgium and northern France were invariably in opposition to the Reichskommissar or governor drawn from the regional Nazi Party leaders, who were personally appointed by Hitler as his representative in each region.

In Holland, the Reichskommissar was the despised Austrian Nazi Arthur Seyss-Inquart; in Norway it was homegrown Nazi Josef Terboven. Belgium and northern France were not given a Reichskommissar until July 1944, when Josef Grohé was appointed to replace the Reichskommissariat, a German civil administration which in turn had succeeded the Military Administration of 1940.

These men acted under Hitler's personal authority and had the power to abolish parliament, dissolve the opposition parties and appoint a Nazi cabinet to govern the country with the assistance of the armed forces and the Gestapo, each of which was generally loathed and distrusted by the other. The leaders were viewed as having been imposed on the people and so became a legitimate target for the resistance.

Sleeping with the enemy – fraternization

> 'The female body represented a combat zone between the
> occupiers and the occupied.'
>
> Anette Warring

Among the 100 to 50,000 victims of the Babi Yar massacres in the
Ukrainian capital Kiev were 100 young women from the local brothels.
They had been murdered in September 1941 by the Germans to erase the
evidence of their own crime: fraternization with women of an 'inferior'
race was explicitly forbidden under the rules of the occupation.

Inevitably, such orders were ignored by men who proved to be highly
selective in regard to which aspects of National Socialist ideology they
chose to adhere to.

The punishment for fraternization was worse for women than for the
soldiers, who were allowed considerable latitude in most cases. Soldiers
were known to be prey to temptation and were spared the consequences
of fathering children with women in the occupied countries, whereas the
women were regarded as having betrayed their country and their men
and accused of bringing shame upon themselves and their community.

As early as May 1940, there were incidents of women having their
heads shaved in public as punishment for being intimate with the enemy
in Norway and, later that summer, in Denmark. Those who carried out
this humiliating treatment did so without fear of reprisals as the Germans
cared nothing for the women. Yet such humiliation did not deter young
girls from seeking intimate and even lasting relationships with enemy
soldiers, though they did so in full knowledge that they would be
ostracized by their families, friends and neighbours, even in the event
that the Germans won the war.

For the conquered people, the Nazis' abuse of their women was
further incitement to hatred and resistance, but that so many women
were willing to cosy up to the Germans was disturbing and was something
their communities could not understand nor forgive.

A moral panic

The absence of so many men was a contributing factor. Husbands, fiancés,
boyfriends, brothers and fathers were either prisoners of war, serving as
forced labourers in Germany, were in hiding or embroiled in the resistance.

Thousands more had either volunteered or had been conscripted into the Waffen-SS, where they wore the uniform of the enemy and swore an oath of loyalty to the foreign dictator. In such cases, many women were left to fend for themselves and if they had children to feed and clothe, they may have felt they had little choice but to seek company from the occupiers. For in place of their men, there were Germans of roughly the same age, who were fit, healthy and in uniform. They had money to spend and were far from home, separated from their wives and girlfriends and craving companionship and sex. In Northern and Western Europe, rape was generally not tolerated. The troops were urged to show restraint and adhere to strict military discipline, but if the local women appeared to be available, they saw no reason to deny themselves what compensation was on offer. Once the initial wariness had worn off, both sides sought normalization of relations to some degree. Fraternization was inevitable though fraught with difficulties.

Spurning the advances of a soldier could result in him forcing himself on an unwilling partner, or reporting her for insulting the Wehrmacht, as happened on numerous occasions, frequently as a means of putting pressure on the woman to be 'sociable'. The increasing incidence of fraternization led to what historian Anette Warring called a 'moral panic' in the occupied countries, which was exacerbated by a significant increase in the spread of venereal disease, illegal terminations and unwanted children fathered by Germans.

Offspring of the Reich

It has been estimated that as many as 12,000 children were fathered by German soldiers in Norway alone and that between 30,000 and 50,000 Norwegian women had long-term relationships with members of the Wehrmacht and other German personnel stationed in the country.

In Denmark, the number of children born of Danish-German parents was closer to 7,500, with up to 50,000 Danish women engaged in intimate relationships with the occupation forces. In France the figure for these illegitimate children may be as high as 200,000. The only other reliable figure we have is for the Netherlands, which is said to have seen between 12,000 and 16,000 children born to Dutch-German parents during the occupation.

In some towns and particularly in rural areas, German soldiers outnumbered the civilians by as many as seven to one, making fraternization more likely. When a soldier was billeted with a local family, initial suspicion sometimes turned to a begrudging trust and even intimacy, despite pressure from the girl's parents for her to resist.

The only contemporary study into the phenomenon was carried out in Copenhagen by a Danish doctor, Grethe Hartmann, between 1943 and 1945. Her 204 subjects had been selected at random from the thousand reported to the Danish police for spreading venereal disease among the Wehrmacht. But Hartmann's study failed to give a true picture of the type of woman who had formed a serious lasting relationship with the Germans because the data included many young women aged between 17 and 25 who were, in the main, prostitutes by profession and so presumably would have had sex with any man who paid. As Anette Warring points out, the soldiers may have named a prostitute to protect the identity of their Danish girlfriends, which reveals more about Danish society's perception of the women 'who had intimate relationships with Germans than it did about the women themselves'. In all the occupied countries there was a reluctance to accept that 'normal', reasonably well-educated women would choose to sleep with the enemy – such an act was thought to belong better to those of a lower intelligence and social class.

In truth, the *tyskerpiger* in Denmark, the *feltmadrasser* in Norway, the *moffenhoer* in Holland and the *femmes à boche* in France were drawn from all backgrounds and did not conform to the stereotypical image of the collaborating 'whore' whom her countrymen denigrated and despised. The only fact that can be stated with certainty was that there were as many motives and attenuating circumstances as there were women.

A recurring theme and one not usually considered or cited is that many women were simply bored and desperate to enliven what was for many a rather dull, mundane existence in small towns and at a bleak and cheerless time of shortages, rationing and oppression. Besides, not all collaborations of this nature were the result of conscious decisions, but simply the consequence of a chance encounter which might have led to a relationship at any other time or place. The resistance of even the staunchest anti-German could be worn down after months of privation and the realization that not all the Boche were 'beasts' or even National Socialists. The war would not last forever and the enemy of today would be a friend tomorrow. It was not uncommon for the more infatuated girl to imagine that she would marry her German lover and live happily with him in Germany when the fighting was over. They justified themselves by citing the popular saying 'love has no will', meaning that they simply couldn't help it.

East and West

German troops were actively encouraged to socialize with women in the Nordic countries of Denmark and Norway as well as in Belgium and Holland, as their populations were believed to be of Aryan ancestry. However, fraternization of any kind was expressly forbidden in the countries of Eastern Europe. And yet, many Germans ignored their orders when it suited them, as proven by the large number of children they sired.

General Walther von Brauchitsch impressed on his German army officers the importance of discipline regarding the men's relationships with civilians in the occupied countries of Northern and Western Europe, especially the women, who were to be treated with respect. He disapproved of the officers who consorted with prostitutes in public and who, by bringing them back to their hotels, tainted the image of the Wehrmacht and their fellow officers.

At times, the Wehrmacht affected a high moral tone, disapproving of the 'loose morals' of certain Danish women who publicly seduced German officers and arranged orgies in their private homes. It was not that the army was concerned with the corruption of its officers so much as the security risk posed by men who might have been inclined to share military secrets to impress their lovers.

Seduction of the young – education and indoctrination

Even the most ardent Nazis could have entertained little hope of converting the adult population in the occupied countries to their cause. The best they could hope for was to turn some disaffected quislings to believe in their cause and to subjugate the rest of the population with a combination of coercion and incentives, hoping that they would fall into line or perhaps even begrudgingly co-operate. Only the children were receptive to indoctrination. Brainwash the young to believe specious party ideology and they could be relied upon to police their parents, relatives and neighbours, to inform on those who dared criticize the regime.

It had worked in Germany but in the occupied countries, the young were not so easily manipulated. For the vast majority, their first loyalty

German troops stroll with wives and girlfriends in occupied France, 1945. French women later paid a terrible price for socializing and sleeping with the enemy.

was naturally to their parents and siblings. When their teachers were replaced by strict, stern-faced zealots and new subjects introduced into the curriculum, the smarter kids smelt a rat.

Across Europe, those teachers who had kept their jobs found themselves having to contradict what they had taught their pupils in the past, particularly with regard to science, geography and history. Younger students may not have noticed that certain textbooks had been withdrawn – specifically, those written by Jewish academics – but they soon noticed that their textbooks had been censored to remove all mention of earlier wars with Germany, particularly the First World War and the Versailles Treaty. French and English language classes were significantly reduced or dropped altogether in favour of German and geography was revised overnight as the map of Europe was redrawn. Entire countries vanished, borders were redrawn and sovereign states renamed to comply with their new status as protectorates of the Greater German Reich.

Scrutinizing students

All schools, colleges and universities in the occupied countries were overseen by the Ministry of Education in Berlin and its various departments. On 8 October 1940, the ministry established a Commission for the Revision of School Manuals to standardize academic textbooks and remove those which were felt to lack 'objectivity', i.e. those which contradicted National Socialism's version of events. In short, the Master Race could not be seen to have been defeated in earlier conflicts and only Aryan heroes, scientists, pioneers and explorers were to be credited with significant advances in the arts and sciences and other fields of human endeavour. Needless to say, no Jews were permitted in the pages of the official texts, which meant the elimination of Einstein, Mendelssohn, Mahler, Niels Bohr, Marx, Trotsky and Disraeli. Leading politicians of the Weimar republic were also banned, such as Walther Rathenau, who had opposed Hitler, as was the French premier, Léon Blum.

But those teachers who believed that they had a responsibility to their profession and their pupils found ways to circumvent the restrictions. A Flemish teacher, Conrad de Meulenaere recalled, 'We could feel that we were closely watched… During class I could allude to the German occupation, for instance by referring to Roman or Greek history. These allusions were well understood by many of my pupils and although some were proponents of the New Order, I was never tattled on.'

De Meulenaere was fortunate. German school inspectors were prone to appearing unannounced to conduct spot checks on classes, scrutinizing pupils' notes and searching for banned books.

Belgian college lecturer Frans Doms remembered:

> We needed to mind our words during class, particularly in the three highest classes when I had to discuss the Latin writers that paralleled with the present political situation. There were always pupil members of New [Order] youth movements. During history class, the situation was even worse. Two times, a German officer came into class to examine our history text-books and ordered the teacher to alter certain passages to present Germany in a positive way, particularly in relation to contemporary history (the '14–'18 war, Treaty of Versailles).

The Second World War was in many respects a war of conflicting ideologies, initially fascism versus democracy, culminating in a triple-sided conflict between fascism, democracy and communism after the invasion of Soviet Russia. This conflict found its counterpart in the classroom, especially in Catholic secondary schools in France and Belgium, where priests taught that National Socialism was ideologically opposed to their credo and the moral principles of the Christian Church.

Soldiers in school

In 1977, the Centre for Historical Research and Documentation on War and Contemporary Society in Brussels found that just over 39 per cent of the priest-teachers they interviewed had experienced direct interference from German authorities in secondary education during the war. In some cases, this meant the occupation of the school by German troops, in others, inspections and intrusive meddling with the curriculum and ultimately the demand for lists of all final year pupils who would be required to report for compulsory labour.

Secondary school students were usually exempt from being drafted because they were under 18, but those who had planned to enter college or university were compelled to report for duty for forced labour. Many teachers ignored the order and some were imprisoned for doing so. Some of the Belgian secondary schools attempted to circumvent the order by adding a seventh year to their institutions' schooling.

German troops were often billeted in boarding schools because of their facilities (dormitories, kitchen facilities and refectories), and where this was the case the staff and pupils were forced to adjust to working and living among them or to find alternative quarters. It was not unknown for the pupils to pester the soldiers, bringing problems for the staff and occasionally, the closure of the school.

But in the end, it was time which proved the Nazis' enemy as the four years of occupation was simply too short a time for their indoctrination to have any lasting effect.

CHAPTER 5
THE NEXT STEP

Romania, Bulgaria, Hungary and Yugoslavia

After the fall of France, Hitler was the undisputed master of Europe, but the conquest of France, Belgium and the Netherlands was only the first step in his plan to create an empire that stretched from Crete to the Caucasus. The next stage was for Nazi Germany to occupy the countries to the east and west as a necessary preliminary for the invasion of Russia. This invasion, code-named Operation Barbarossa, would prove to be Hitler's undoing – just as it had with the 'Little Corporal', Napoleon, a century before. However, by 1942, the Third Reich would dominate a land-mass larger than the United States, 'one which was more densely populated and more economically productive than any in the world'.

Although Bulgaria, Hungary and Romania had declared themselves allies of the Nazi state, Hitler knew he could not rely on them to put up much of a fight if the war turned against them. He believed the Russians were demoralized and would not resist an attack, as Stalin had recently executed hundreds of high-ranking officers in another mad purge. The Wehrmacht had only to kick down the door, as he put it, and the 'whole rotten mess would collapse'. The British were still licking their wounds after Dunkirk and were in no fit state to mount a second front, but he could not be certain that they would stay inactive for long, or that the Americans would remain neutral. It was therefore imperative that these so-called Axis powers be brought into line to actively support the German war effort.

Hungary had in abundance grain, oil and bauxite, an ore used in the petrochemical industry and the production of aluminium, essential for the manufacture of aeroplanes. Romania also had grain and oil to fuel the German war machine. Both countries bordered Russia and would be needed to launch the invasion of the Soviet Union. Plans were drawn up for the invasion of Romania in anticipation of the country changing sides, but it was never occupied. Both Romania and Hungary would also supply hundreds of thousands of men to fight for the Reich on the Eastern Front. Hungary alone provided 400,000 men of whom fewer than 60,000 returned home after the war. In exchange for their support, Hungary regained territory taken by the Allies after the First World War.

Wilful submission

Romania was ruled by King Michael, whose youth and inexperience led him to listen to the advice of his Machiavellian General Ion Antonescu, a devotee of Hitler. Bulgaria was ruled by Tsar Boris III, who made no effort to hide his admiration for the German dictator.

Antonescu appointed members of the anti-Semitic far-right Iron Guard Party to the government before joining the Axis alliance in November 1940. The Romanian army and police forces would collaborate with the Nazis in exterminating the country's Jews, but they also instigated pogroms of their own, resulting in the murder of 160,000 Jews. An additional 420,000 Romanian Jews died in the Holocaust after having been transported to extermination and concentration camps beyond the country's borders.

Bulgaria willingly turned over its naval facilities on the Black Sea at Varna and Burgas to serve as bases for German U-boats, which would be crucial for subduing the threat posed to German supply lines by Russian battleships.

Yugoslavia was occupied almost as an afterthought. At the time this perennially unstable country was riven by internal strife and was expected to align itself with the Allies, but it was isolated geographically and so Hitler included the seizure of Yugoslavia in his plans to occupy Greece. On 6 April 1941, German, Italian and Hungarian troops occupied Yugoslavia and partitioned the country between them, allocating a share to Bulgaria and providing arms to the pro-fascist Ustashi, the Croatian separatists.

HUNGARY – 20 November 1940

'Hungary found itself in the crossfire of an increasingly aggressive Nazi régime in Germany as well as a menacing and powerful Soviet Union. First allies then enemies, the Nazi and Soviet dictatorships began a life-and-death fight to create a new European system of client and subordinated states, where there was no room for an independent Hungary.'

Memorial at the House of Terror, Budapest

When Regent of Hungary Miklós Horthy was sidelined in March 1944, after a failed attempt to reach a separate peace with the Allies, Hungarian fascist Ferenc Szálasi, leader of the Arrow Cross Party, was installed as its puppet premier. German troops to the number of 120,000 occupied the country to enforce his authority. This single act has remained the basis of Hungary's persistent claim to have been a victim of Nazi aggression, a reluctant ally forced into the arms of the German dictator after having been cruelly abandoned to its fate by the French and British at Munich and by Churchill and Roosevelt's declaration of solidarity with Stalin in the summer of 1941.

The revisionists and apologists further claim that the Nazis double-crossed their Hungarian allies by deliberately sending them to their certain deaths in the fiercest fighting on the Don, refusing them transport and shelter during the retreat and leaving them to freeze to death in what one Hungarian commentator called 'a tragic, but retro-actively glorious Bolshevik crusade'.

Hungary fights back

Although the leaders of the Axis countries had made a pact with Hitler, their people had not.

Pupils in Budapest were taught that British bombers had destroyed the elegant Apollo cinema in the Újpest district, when in fact it had been the work of the Hungarian resistance. During the occupation, the building had been used as a headquarters for the Arrow Cross, the Hungarian Nazi Party, who brought their victims there to be interrogated. Many were tortured and executed, their bodies thrown into the Danube. Some were still breathing.

In late 1944, members of the Hungarian resistance arrived dressed in Nazi uniforms and demanded that the prisoners be handed over to be executed. Acting in haste, they left behind their luggage for safekeeping, promising to return as soon as they had dealt with their prisoners. But just minutes later there was a devastating explosion, killing several Nazis and gravely wounding many more. The suitcases had contained enough explosives to demolish the front of the iconic building.

Such courageous acts were practically unknown up until that point because the Soviet regime suppressed all accounts of resistance with the exception of those carried out by card-carrying communists. According to Hungarian historian Thomas Land:

> Contrary to popular perception, there was a great deal of spectacular, albeit often ineffective, resistance to the Nazi order. Thousands of forged identity documents were in circulation. Such papers saved me and some of my family. Groups of Zionists, students, workers, army deserters and other outraged patriots rescued captives, blew up military installations and eventually prevented the destruction of vital civilian infrastructure by the retreating Nazis.

The Battle for Budapest

The Battle for Budapest raged for 50 days from 29 December 1944 to 13 February 1945 and was compared by some military historians to the Battle of Stalingrad in its intensity and carnage. But unlike Stalingrad, the house-to-house fighting in the Hungarian capital was fought with the civilian population of 800,000 caught in the crossfire between the Red Army, the Germans and its Romanian allies. It was the hellish climax to four years of tyranny, which left 40,000 civilians dead, the majority of them women and children. Seventeen thousand of these people were Jews who starved to death or died of disease in the ghetto.

Ironically, more Jews would have been murdered by the Hungarian fascists if it had not been for a German officer, Colonel-General Gerhard Schmidhuber of the 13th Panzer Division. He was acting under orders from his superior, Karl Pfeffer-Wildenbruch, the German Commander of Budapest. Wildenbruch was not a hardened Nazi and, as a former policeman, he had been trained to protect his prisoners. He stationed troops at the gates of the ghetto to deter the Arrow Cross paramilitaries from massacring the surviving inhabitants.

Hungary was liberated by the Russians on 4 April 1945. It had exchanged one dictatorship for another.

The Hungarian Holocaust

Hungary's dictator Rear-Admiral Miklós Horthy had aligned himself with Hitler in the belief that Nazism was the lesser of two evils, the other being communism with which he was morbidly obsessed. But Horthy was more than sympathetic to Hitler's racial policies and had himself enacted a number of anti-Semitic laws – more than 300 in total – from the earliest years of his reign, which had begun in 1920. Hungary was the first country in Europe to pass anti-Jewish laws. Such legislation paved the way for the first mass murder of Hungarian Jews in August 1941, shortly after Hungary entered the war, when 20,000 men, women and children were deported to German-occupied Ukraine where they were murdered by the SS.

In March 1944, when the Red Army massed on Hungary's eastern border and the defeat of Nazi Germany seemed inevitable, the Hungarian government sanctioned the deportation of half a million Jews to Auschwitz, an operation which was accomplished in just 56 days. This impressed Adolf Eichmann, who had been sent by his SS superiors to co-ordinate the round-up and deportation of the Jews from Budapest:

> The deportation experts who came to Hungary with Adolf Eichmann after the German occupation in March 1944 consisted of less than 200 people. The guarantee of success could not [have been achieved without] the collaboration of the Hungarian authorities. [With the help of the entire Hungarian civil service, around 51,000 people, and the active participation of close to 200,000 civilians, this small group of extermination experts accomplished the deportation of all the Jewish population of the countryside in less than two months.] In fifty-six days[!] – according to German documents

> – 437,402 Jews were deported by 147 trains, with the exception of 15,000, to Auschwitz.

One of Eichmann's deputies commented at the time, 'It seems the Hungarians are indeed the descendants of the Huns; we would never have managed so well without them.'

There was only one dissenting voice – that of Rudolf Höss, the commandant of Auschwitz, who complained that his men could not 'process' so many victims and that the crematoria were already working to capacity. The Hungarians pressed him to accept six trainloads of Jews a day, but had to be content with shipping no more than four, each carrying 3,000 people.

Every third Jew murdered in Auschwitz was Hungarian and yet, the Hungarians would subsequently present themselves as victims of Nazi aggression. However, the facts suggest that they were more than willing participants in the Final Solution.

BULGARIA – 1 March 1941

Faced with certain defeat by Hitler's formidable war machine, Bulgaria's dictator Tsar Boris III made a pact with Nazi Germany. On 1 March 1941, Bulgaria joined the Axis and invited German military 'observers' into the country so that they could prepare for the planned invasion of the Soviet Union the following spring. In return, Germany promised to restore the Bulgarian territory that had been surrendered to Greece and Turkey after 1918. But to the Tsar's surprise and anger, his subjects were not willing to collude with their ruler, especially when it came to handing over the country's 50,000 Jews.

Bulgaria had no history of endemic anti-Semitism. Moreover, there was a general feeling among the population that the Jews had shared in their suffering under the oppressive Saxe-Coburg dynasty and were deserving of their sympathy and protection. As soon as the first anti-Jewish measures were announced, depriving Bulgaria's Jews of their citizenship and their rights, mass street protests were organized.

The Orthodox Church considered it their Christian duty to oppose an 'unjust' law that was 'not in the interests of the nation'. Its opposition was soon echoed by professional bodies representing doctors, scientists and lawyers.

The Academy of Sciences objected on the grounds that the reference to a 'pure race' in the bill was a 'mystification' and would be an indelible stain on the 'culture and dignity of the Bulgarian people'.

Once these respected bodies declared themselves against the persecution of the Jews, there was a wave of public outrage. Parliament was deluged with thousands of letters from incensed citizens and workers' groups. But the Tsar and his pro-Nazi ministers would not be swayed. Even rumours of a coup by senior army officers could not dissuade them from ratifying the Law for the Protection of the Nation on 8 October 1940. Tsar Boris believed the Germans would assist them in enforcing the law, but the protests continued despite the threat posed by the Germans, who were now on Bulgarian soil in force.

Opposition parties and the underground anti-fascist Fatherland Front instigated a campaign to inform the population of what fate awaited the Jews. They were already being evicted from their homes, dismissed from their jobs and ordered to wear a yellow star in public. It was only a matter of time before they would be rounded up and transported to a slave labour or concentration camp.

The guerrilla force

But it was not only the persecution of their Jewish neighbours that stirred up resentment towards Tsar Boris and his Nazi friends. The underground press and radio informed their incredulous listeners that the intelligentsia would be the next group to be eliminated, after which the armed forces would see a purge of their officers and the unions would be abolished and workers enslaved.

When the first deportation of Jews was announced on 24 May 1943, thousands poured on to the streets of the capital to voice their anger and demonstrate their solidarity with their Jewish neighbours: 'Take your stand before your neighbouring Jewish homes and do not let them be led away by force!' declared the underground broadcasts. 'Hide the children and do not give them to the executioners! Crowd the Jewish quarters and manifest your solidarity with the oppressed Jews!'

They did more than that. They marched on the Royal Palace, demanding the law be repealed. Fearing a revolution, the Tsar ordered the police to attack the protestors and arrest the ringleaders, but the crowd would not be silenced. Boris was forced to back down and rescind the order to deport the first shipment of Jews.

The Ceremony of the Taking Down of the Olympic Flag, 1936 – from right:
Hermann Goering, Joseph Goebbels, Adolf Hitler, Tsar Boris III, General August
von Mackenson and Wilhelm Frick. Tsar Boris was high up on Hitler's guest list.

The opposition to the pro-Nazi regime continued to gather momentum with acts of sabotage directed against German forces and government buildings. The resistance saw a substantial increase in recruitment until it could offer an effective opposition to the Bulgarian army and their German allies. In fact, the guerrilla force was so strong that the Germans were forced to retain a significant number of men in the country to fight it, preventing them from being deployed to the Russian Front as had been hoped. Of the 20,000 guerrillas, 260 were Jews, whose contribution to the fight against fascism has been commemorated in the naming of streets in their honour.

GREECE – April 1941–autumn 1944

It is impossible to talk of 'daily life' in Nazi-occupied Greece as if we were speaking of life in occupied Holland, France or Denmark. Under Nazi tyranny, the Greek people suffered a relentless series of atrocities and brutality that made routine life intolerable and unfeasible.

During the German occupation of Greece, an estimated 50,000 civilians were murdered and a further 450,000 starved to death as a direct result of Nazi policy to reduce the inhabitants' will and ability to resist. In addition, 60,000 Greek Jews were transported to concentration camps, thereby eradicating a culture that had thrived on the Aegean for generations.

In total, an estimated 578,000 Greeks perished, almost five times as many as the Russians lost in terms of a percentage of the population.

Malnutrition saw the incidence of tuberculosis rise to 80 per cent in children, while starvation left many women barren, though it has to be said that the famine was exacerbated by the Allied blockade that prevented the transportation of essential supplies through the Aegean.

The Germans' irrational enmity for the Greeks saw more than 2,000 villages razed to the ground and industrial sites, including the textile and chemical factories of Athens, Salonika and Eleusis, gutted. The Nazis' pitiless treatment of the Greeks stemmed from their spite at the fierce resistance put up by the 50,000 freedom fighters of the communist Greek People's Liberation Army (ELAS) and their unlikely allies in the right-wing National Republican Greek League (EDES).

From 1942, the Greek resistance grew substantially, until its forces were able to drive the Germans out of certain areas. They had great success in the mountains, where they could rely on sympathetic villagers to shelter them and share their meagre provisions, while the mountains themselves provided hiding places where the guerrillas could stockpile weapons. In their rage, the Germans slaughtered livestock and destroyed vineyards, as well as crops of wheat, barley and beans and other basic necessities. Donkeys, sheep, goats, hogs and poultry were butchered and left to rot so that the people would have no meat, milk or cheese. Destruction was systematic and deliberate.

They then turned to the infrastructure, blowing up the main harbours, shipping canals, bridges and roads and setting fire to a quarter of the country's forests. Water treatment plants and sewage works were demolished so that the population were reduced to primitive subsistence level, the telephone network was torn up and both private and public transport was rendered unusable. Three-quarters of Greek shipping was sunk or rendered unseaworthy.

Italy's revenge

> 'For the sake of historical truth, I must verify that only the Greeks, of all the adversaries who confronted us, fought with bold courage and highest disregard of death.'
>
> Adolf Hitler, speech to the Reichstag, 4 May 1941

The Germans might never have invaded had the Greeks not beaten back the Italians in October 1940. The Italians had underestimated the Greeks' determination to defend their homeland and appeared ignorant of the fact that the Greek army was well prepared to repel an invasion.

The humiliating rout of Mussolini's forces, which were forced all the way back to Albania, led Hitler to intercede on his allies' behalf and by 27 April, Athens had fallen and the swastika had been raised over the Acropolis.

Once the Greek army had been defeated, the Free Greek government had fled to Alexandria and the partisans had taken to the hills, the Germans divided the region between themselves and their Axis allies, the Italians and the Bulgarians.

The Italians seized the opportunity to take revenge on the Greeks by killing all the livestock they couldn't carry away. But they were frequently outsmarted by the villagers, who retreated en masse into the mountains until the invaders had gone.

In the mountain caves and monasteries, the displaced people established hospitals and schools, educating the children and performing plays that underlined what it meant to be Greek, so that they would grow up to join the resistance.

Greece's occupation may have seemed to be an insignificant episode strategically speaking, but it was crucial to the outcome of the entire war. The diversion of German resources delayed the planned invasion of Russia by a month – a critical delay, as it turned out, for the Russian winter set in before the Germans could take Moscow. As British Foreign Secretary Anthony Eden observed:

> [Greece] was the motive for the revolution in Yugoslavia… she held the Germans in the mainland and in Crete for six weeks… she upset the chronological order of all German High Command's plans and thus brought a general reversal of the entire course of the war.

The Unwanted

The recent discovery of letters written by German soldiers stationed in Greece, Crete and the Aegean islands during the Second World War reveal that not all of the invaders were hardened Nazis and that a minority were even actively supportive of the oppressed population. A few were so enraged by the atrocities they witnessed that they deserted and joined the partisans.

As many as 500 soldiers from the penal battalions, commonly known as the Unwanted, were either anti-fascists who had been imprisoned by the Nazis or former criminals with no particular liking for Hitler's regime.

The local population were naturally wary of German soldiers claiming to be anti-fascist, but those who managed to convince the inhabitants of their sincerity proved to be valuable sources of information concerning troop movements, shipments of supplies and the acquisition of weapons. Two hundred of these men were discovered, arrested and executed as spies.

The Germans formed penal battalions in Italy, France, Belgium, Bulgaria, Albania and Yugoslavia, each with 1,000 men, but the number of the Unwanted in Greece was greater than in any of the other occupied or Nazi puppet states, with an estimated 17,000 Greek men fighting under the Nazi banner.

CHAPTER 6
NAZI EMPIRE IN THE EAST

UKRAINE – 22 June 1941

> 'In three hundred years, the country will be one of the loveliest gardens in the world. As for the natives, we'll have to screen them carefully. The Jew, that destroyer, we shall drive out... Our colonizing penetration must be constantly progressive, until it reaches the stage where our own colonists far outnumber the local inhabitants.'
>
> Adolf Hitler, October 1941

Hitler's vision of an occupied Europe was radically different from that visualized by his predecessors. The Kaiser had had ambitions to extend the third-largest empire in the modern world to accommodate a rapidly increasing population and stem the mass migration of German colonists who, it was feared, would lose their national identity through assimilation. The colonies would provide cheap labour and their natural resources and industry would be exploited; as such, they would be developed and modernized and the population would benefit to some degree by the investment and industrialization. The people would be governed by Germany, but the empire would not intrude in their culture, customs or religious practices.

Hitler, however, had no intention of allowing the local inhabitants of the conquered territories to the east to profit from the process or to share its benefits. He would never countenance trade with the inhabitants. The Führer's vision was a malign and corrupted version of imperialism. He was set on exploiting the indigenous workforce and plundering their countries' resources. He planned to eradicate those he considered racially 'inferior' and enslave the rest of the population. The occupied countries of Eastern Europe would become vast labour camps, where German settlers would rule over the inhabitants as the Egyptians had ruled over their slaves in the time of the Pharaohs.

It would be what American historian Wendy Lower called an 'Aryan paradise', or the extreme realization of a 'German colonial fantasy'. Lower finds it revealing that Hitler, Himmler and Alfred Rosenberg (head of the Reich Ministry for the Occupied Eastern Territories) all referred to the American pioneers, the British Empire and the colonization of Africa in their speeches and writings to justify their own imperial ambitions in Eastern Europe.

Blut und Boden

Nazi colonization was to be undertaken over a period of 20 years as part of a long-term campaign of *Blut und Boden* (race and space) to civilize the East and Germanize those deemed worthy of assimilation into the Reich. Hitler was also determined to avenge himself on those races who had – in his mind – persecuted generations of Germans throughout history and had driven them eastwards, for example, during the great exodus of the 19th century when German Catholics, Baptists and Mennonites fled to Poland and Russia. The past suffering of the German people was the underlying rationale for Hitler's drive eastwards, with the historic acts of certain nations determining how well the population of these countries were now to be treated by their Nazi conquerors.

Hitler had been strongly influenced by Karl Haushofer, a leading proponent of geopolitics and former professor of Deputy Führer Rudolf Hess. Haushofer stressed the importance of human migration as a means of revitalizing a race that might otherwise stagnate if confined within its own borders. If the Aryans were to preserve their 'racial superiority', it was imperative that they colonize the East and, by doing so, fulfil their destiny.

Such ideas had been outlined in the 25 Point Plan of the National Socialist German Workers' Party (NSDAP) manifesto in 1920, long before Hitler joined. But in seizing on this idea, Hitler tapped into a widely held belief among Germans that they were destined to be masters of Europe and that providence would lead them to the victory they had been so cruelly denied in 1918.

The countries of Eastern Europe were to be the battleground in what was a racial war of ideals as much as a military conquest. Hitler and his advisers could not envisage the arid lands of Africa as their *völkisch* utopia and so they looked to Eastern Europe, initially to Ukraine, to fulfil their immediate needs. Ukraine was vast and fertile, at that time producing a quarter of the wheat consumed by the Soviet Union, thus earning itself the title 'the bread-basket of Europe'. All that needed to be done was to displace the Slavs who lived there.

Soldier-peasants

The Nazis saw the Slavs as ill-educated, simple-minded savages who could be bought with a handful of glass beads. The colonists would be 'soldier-peasants', who would cultivate the land with a loaded rifle at their side, in the manner of the early American pioneers' defence of land from Native American tribes.

During a tour of the region in August 1941, Hitler set out his vision:

> The German colonist ought to live on handsome, spacious farms. The German services will be lodged in marvellous buildings, the governors in palaces... What India was for England the territories of Russia will be for us. If only I could make the German people understand what this space means for our future! Colonies are a precarious possession, but this ground is safely ours. Europe is not a geographic entity; it's a racial entity.

Hitler viewed the indigenous population as inherently cruel and barbaric, supported by testimony from publications such as Ludwig Alsdorf's *Indien*, which offered an excruciatingly detailed account of Britain's exploitation of India and an unfavourable portrayal of the Native Americans, the Incas and the Indians.

Rosenberg and Himmler were also taken with Alsdorf's endorsement of the way the British treated the 'natives' in India. Just prior to the Nazi invasion of Ukraine in June 1941, Rosenberg approved the book for all Nazi commissars in the region, while in a speech at Zhytomyr that year, Himmler exhorted his men to learn from the example set by the British in India. It was the SS Reichsführer's belief that a single German colonist could rule 100,000 Ukrainians by the sheer force of his superior personality, never mind the terror organization that stood behind him in the shadows.

*German soldiers queue up for rations from a mobile canteen in lower Ukraine,
July 1941.*

The *Untermenschen*

However, Hitler's empire in the East would differ from the British model in several significant respects. Firstly, the white settler saw himself as the 'moderate' civilizing influence in India and in Britain's other colonies, whereas Hitler believed the Slavs were *Untermenschen* (sub-humans) and therefore not capable of being civilized, nor deserving of help. In Hitler's view, the Ukrainians possessed no sense of self-respect, community or obligation to the state. They were, in his words, 'unsanitary savages'. Education was wasted on them, as was health care. Other than those deemed fit for manual labour and those individuals who exhibited 'Aryan' characteristics, the Ukrainians were to be denied even the most basic amenities and assistance, such as inoculations against disease, in the hope that they would all die out.

When the first German units reached the Ukrainian heartland, they had every reason to believe the lies they had been told by the party leaders. Stalin's policies had reduced the population to subsistence level. They lived as their ancestors must have done – in spartan wooden houses, with no sanitation, running water, power or even windows to keep out the cold. Their lot was little better than that of their livestock and yet their farms boasted modern tractors and grain silos that would have cost several times their annual income.

For generations, the Ukrainians had lived alongside Russians, Poles, ethnic Germans and some even tolerated the Jews. But when the Germans came, they turned on their neighbours in the belief that the Germans would reward them by treating them fairly and giving them well-paid work.

They were soon disillusioned.

Aktions

At first, the Ukrainians naively provided all the information the invaders requested as to who lived in their village or town and where they were to be found. They presented themselves to the Nazi officials in the hope of finding work and offered their documents as proof of their identity. Within weeks, the military administration had all the information they needed to begin rounding up their political opponents, the 'undesirable' racial elements (specifically the Romanies and the Jews) and many Soviet prisoners of war who had been abandoned in the rout of the Red Army.

It had been Hitler's stated intent to purge Eastern Europe of Bolshevism, by which he meant the Jews as well as the communists. But few outside the Nazi leadership understood the implications until the exterminations began in the summer of 1941. Earlier that year, Hitler had ordered Himmler and Göring to form execution squads (the *Einsatzgruppen*) from the ranks of the SS and brief them as to how they were to identify, isolate and execute political commissars and the intelligentsia.

At the same time, the army was given a free hand to eliminate any individual or group who was thought to pose a threat to the advancing troops. Every member of the suspect's family and even whole villages would also be liable for summary execution as they would be considered guilty by association. This effectively condoned all reprisals and meant that those accused of participating in mass killings would not be answerable to a military court. This decree, issued on 13 May 1941, absolved all members of the German armed forces who would take part in atrocities and would give them the right to murder with impunity.

As Field Marshal Walter von Reichenau, commander of the Sixth Army, stated in a memo dated October 1941, the German soldier should be 'the bearer of a ruthless national ideology'. He was soon handing out combat medals to those who had proved uncommonly efficient in eliminating 'Jewish subhuman elements' and POWs near Zhytomyr.

It had not occurred to the Nazis that the thousands they killed might have been more usefully employed in the massive construction programmes that required a huge workforce and that their manpower shortage could have been solved if they had not been so determined to implement their genocidal racial policy.

'Cleansing' the region of partisans and 'pacification' became a convenient pretext for random wholesale slaughter as there were few organized guerrilla groups active at that time. When rare and isolated acts of sabotage were carried out by Ukrainians, the blame was invariably put on the Jews to justify the mass killings and to appease the majority of Ukrainians who were co-operating with the occupation forces.

Sizeable numbers of Red Army deserters and civilian refugees were sheltering in the forests and remote villages outside the cities of Zhytomyr, Vinnytsia and Berdychiv, but they posed no threat to the Germans. However, the Ukrainian auxiliaries kept themselves busy and ingratiated themselves with their Nazi paymasters by claiming the forests were crawling with 'armed Russian gangs' whom they volunteered to seek out and destroy. The Germans appear to have taken reports of 'enemies behind the lines' with some scepticism, but nevertheless sent execution squads to investigate and carry out more 'cleansing' *Aktions*, partly to reassure their superiors that they were being thorough.

As the American historian John-Paul Himka observes:

> In normal historical situations, active sadists would be marginalized as criminal elements and latent ones would not become active... But during the Nazi occupation of Ukraine, criminality moved from the margins of society to its center, and individuals with an inclination to rob, extort, and kill were not lost in the larger crowd of humanity, but rather stepped to the fore.

POWs

The Germans had more immediate problems on their hands – the vast numbers of Russian POWs. There were tens of thousands to be interned, supervised and fed, far too many as far as the German High Command was concerned. After the German victory at Kiev in September 1941, 600,000 Soviet troops surrendered. Kiev was less than 100 miles (161 km) from Zhytomyr. Subsequently, German transit camps frequently saw numbers comparable to the population of the nearest town, yet they had inadequate provisions to feed their prisoners and no clothing or medical supplies to spare. The Wehrmacht had other priorities, as the fighting was intensifying in the push eastwards. Their solution was simple – they would leave the prisoners to starve or die of wilful neglect in unheated, overcrowded, pestiferous camps. As Quartermaster-General Eduard Wagner stated, 'The more prisoners that die, the better off we are.'

The Soviet government had refused to sign the Geneva covenant of 1929, so the German High Command felt under no obligation to treat their prisoners humanely. Wendy Lower cites the case of the camp at Berdychiv, Dulag-205, where the mortality rate was a staggering 82 per cent. On the outskirts of the historic city at Krasnaya Gora, thousands of POWs were shot by the Wehrmacht, giving lie to the belief that it was only the SS who carried out atrocities in the East.

By December 1941, Gestapo chief Heinrich Müller could boast of having eliminated 16,000 of the 22,000 POWs in General Reinicke's region (the greater part of which was in Ukraine), many of whom had been 'shot while attempting to escape'. Thousands more had died on the forced marches from the battlefield to the camps.

The Soviets' legacy

When the Russians abandoned central and eastern Ukraine in the eye of the German advance in the summer of 1941, they had left a feudal society reminiscent of those in Europe during the Middle Ages. The main roads were little more than dirt tracks, with many people getting around by horse and cart, bicycle or simply on foot. Much of the ageing railway network that connected the major towns and cities had been destroyed in the fighting. The telephone system was confined to the urban centres and unreliable. In rural areas, the primary sources of information were newspapers and even rumour, as most of the wireless sets were owned by the more affluent and educated inhabitants of the towns and cities.

When the Germans invaded few able-bodied men under 60 were to be seen. Many had either been conscripted into the Red Army or had been forced to leave their homes to work in the industrial towns to the east. Many more had been murdered or imprisoned during Stalin's purges. Those men who remained worked mainly in menial jobs and were often suspected of having avoided conscription so that they could provide intelligence to their Soviet paymasters. They were among the first to be killed.

Rural communities consisted mainly of the elderly, the unfit, women and children. The women worked the farms and tended the children; as such, when the Germans freed their men from abandoned Soviet prison camps, many greeted the invaders as liberators. They had suffered a decade of Soviet oppression and were embittered witnesses to Stalin's scorched-earth policy which saw their villages, livestock, crops and grain stores destroyed by the retreating Russians.

The agents of Satan

The Germans presented themselves as liberators, dropping leaflets and nailing up posters proclaiming the end of the 'Jewish-Bolshevik tyranny'. Ukrainian nationalists dared to hope of independence and took the Germans' proclamation promising freedom of worship as a sign that they would soon be determining their own affairs under German supervision.

Clerics emerged from hiding and the churches were reopened. Reconstruction of the buildings began in earnest and with renewed hope. But as Wendy Lower notes in her study *Nazi Empire-Building and the Holocaust in the Ukraine*, many religious ceremonies were hijacked by extreme nationalist and anti-Semitic priests to incite racial hatred against the Jews, who they blamed for all their ills.

Anti-Semitism was so deep-rooted that former neighbours, workers and classmates willingly informed on the Jews to curry favour with the military administration.

Nina Glozman survived the Holocaust but only after several miraculous escapes. At one point, she found work in a sugar factory but was recognized by a former classmate and denounced to the Germans. It was only thanks to the intervention of a fellow factory worker that she managed to flee to safety.

After the massacre of Jews in Khmil'nyk, locals held a church service to give thanks to God for their deliverance from the 'agents of Satan'.

Lower notes that Ukrainians and ethnic Germans soon learned how to 'play the Jewish card' for the favour of the military administration, improving their conditions and settling personal scores in the process. It seems fair to say that if the nationalists did not actively incite pogroms against their former Jewish neighbours, then they were, at the very least, indifferent to their plight.

Ukrainian collaborators

The Germans encouraged the nationalists to spread false hopes of a Ukrainian independent state and trained them to fight alongside the SS and the Wehrmacht for the onslaught against Soviet Russia. The unsuspecting activists returned to their villages and began to organize paramilitary youth groups and cultural activities with the aim of garnering support for the nationalist cause. They found willing accomplices for the inhabitants were close to starvation, their workplaces having been destroyed by the Soviets during their retreat and provisions severely depleted. The inhabitants of one village were reduced to sustaining themselves with only milk as there was no bread, meat or potatoes, which had been their staple diet.

By the autumn of 1941, it was clear that the Germans had no intention of conferring power on the Ukrainians. Instead, they appointed local ethnic Germans in positions of authority, regardless of their ability. Many were uneducated labourers and their Ukrainian neighbours resented being commanded by men they had no respect for. They also begrudged the preferential treatment afforded the *Volksdeutsche*, as they were commonly known, who were given hot meals by the German army. In the view of the Nazi leadership, the ethnic Germans were 'victims of Judeo-Bolshevism', Lower notes, while the Ukrainians thought of them as 'a nuisance and a threat'.

Lower cites the case of a Vinnytsia baker, Theodor Kitzmann, who was employed in the office of the German field commander and then promoted to district leader in the civil administration with the power of life and death over 30,000 inhabitants in 40 villages.

Those deemed unsuitable to hold official posts were drafted into the police as auxiliaries and took active part in the massacre of Jews and other atrocities. The Germans demonstrated a preference for employing Ukrainians over their own people, whom they considered untrustworthy and less docile. Ukrainian collaborators were thought to be more conscientious and eager to please their superiors as both shared a loathing for the Jews and the Poles, the second largest ethnic minority in the country and long-time enemy of the Ukrainians.

A Ukrainian militia was formed but they were to be armed only with clubs and knives. Evidently, the Germans did not extend their trust to furnishing them with loaded weapons.

One militia man was to provide 'security' for every ten households, which was a Nazi euphemism for intimidation, to make it known that the locals lived under the watchful eye of their paid thugs.

The *Schutzmannschaften*

The 'honeymoon' with the Germans ended abruptly that autumn with the imposition of curfews, the levying of a tax on livestock, travel restrictions (villagers could not venture beyond the boundary of their village without written permission) and the imposition of the death penalty for looters. With so many abandoned dwellings, the temptation to steal in such a time of dire need was overwhelming for some.

But for the nationalists, it was the prohibition on the possession of weapons that proved to be the divisive act. The German policy of collective guilt meant that an entire village would be held responsible if one of their number was found in possession of illegal weapons and the Germans did not make idle threats. Meanwhile, German soldiers looted freely, leaving the inhabitants to look on with envy and soon their initial joy at being 'liberated' turned very sour indeed. In towns and cities, Ukrainians were banned from using their own public transport, food rationing was introduced with extra rations for those who worked for the occupation and certain shops were designated for Germans only.

The Ukrainians got the message that their German masters did not think very highly of them. Members of the auxiliary police (*Schutzmannschaften*) were frequently reprimanded for being unreliable, ill-disciplined, shiftless and disorganized. They were also accused of corrupting German officials by offering to provide items on the black market and stealing from the military stores that they had been sent to guard. But then what did the Germans expect if they were not paid? Their loyalty had been bought with the promise of three hot meals a day and a roof over their heads in a shared barracks. Most of the 6,000 auxiliaries were not even given uniforms and none were issued with weapons. All they had was a wooden club and an armband to identify them as collaborators. However, they now had status of a sort, instead of being derided nobodies. Those who operated in the civilian zones were under the command of Reichsführer-SS Heinrich Himmler and, as such, were feared by their former neighbours. They relished the power they now had over their fellow countrymen and they abused it at every opportunity. They could preside over their neighbours and force farmers and factory workers to increase productivity or face the consequences. These were not career policemen, but the dregs of society who were incapable and unqualified to do anything else.

Those recruited by army commanders in the military zones came under the authority of the individual regional commanders and were typically recruited through newspaper advertisements and public appeals.

Useless eaters

By the spring of 1942, it was clear the Germans would not tolerate more talk of Ukrainian independence. They had arrested all the local leaders of the nationalist movement to avoid dissent. That settled, the Ukrainians were assigned simple tasks such as organizing emergency services, clearing rubble, restoring water and power and providing produce for the street markets. Public services such as post offices and banks were up and running again, but the transport system was still in chaos, the infrastructure and the rolling stock having been destroyed by the retreating Red Army and during German air raids.

The ethnic Germans were favoured with loans and credit schemes and offered administrative positions at military bases, while the most demeaning jobs were given to the Jews, who were further humiliated by the imposition of a punitive 'tax' for allegedly 'stealing' goods that they exchanged with local farmers for food. But at least they were still at liberty, for the moment. The disabled and mentally ill had been categorized as 'useless eaters' and quietly eliminated by wilful neglect and lethal injection as part of the Nazi Euthanasia Programme.

Rayonchef

The Nazis were thorough and methodical. They were determined that not a single 'undesirable' should escape their clutches. With that end in mind, they established an army command post in every village to secure the area and to ensure orderly management of resources. These military commanders immediately sought out Ukrainians to serve as district leaders to whom they could delegate responsibility for seeing that their orders were implemented.

These *Rayonchef* (district leaders) were aware that they were being handed a poisoned chalice, but they had no choice other than to accept. With the authority of the German military commanders behind them, they could rule their designated district like feudal lords, but they were accountable to the Germans. Failure to fulfil their task meant their tenure and their lives could be terminated permanently. Their names were circulated on posters and public notices for all to see. They became targets for partisans, Soviet deserters and anyone else who resented the presence of the occupation army and they would not be permitted to carry a gun to defend themselves.

They were selected from among the better-educated professional class: teachers, clerics, doctors, etc. and were generally middle-aged so they had a wide experience of local life under the previous Soviet administration and even back to the First World War. But they were willing and capable, if a tad inclined to take it easy.

As Wendy Lower observes, they had lost a sense of urgency and initiative, having been exposed to the Soviet system for too long. The Germans had to goad them into action and could not afford to leave them unsupervised for long.

The Nazis among them devised simple, crude tests to see if the men they had chosen were of the right temperament to be community 'elders'. In Popil'nia, one candidate was ordered to beat one of his neighbours. It can safely be assumed that this was not an isolated incident.

The alternative was hard labour and there was more than enough of that to go around with reconstruction projects, agriculture and transportation links needing manual workers by the thousand. Those who were not willing to work, or were unable to work, starved. Ration cards were reserved for those who earned them. The Germans felt no obligation to feed anyone but those who served the Fatherland. As Lower states: 'The genocidal bloodbath that marked the onset of German rule over Zhytomyr developed from a lethal mix of Nazi racial policies, Prusso-German militarism, and an arrogant "Final Solution" approach to problem-solving and empire-building.'

CHAPTER 7
JEWISH RESISTANCE IN NAZI-OCCUPIED EUROPE

Resistance in the occupied countries assumed many forms, not all of them violent. Courageous individuals assisted thousands of Jews to escape transportation to concentration camps in defiance of the edicts that forbade anyone offering them aid or assistance. Others facilitated the publication and distribution of underground newspapers, the performance of banned plays, the organizing of concerts and even exhibitions of 'degenerate art' under the very noses of the Nazis to foster solidarity and raise morale.

There were no ghettos in Western Europe and few laws restricting their movements, although Jews were confined to certain districts and subject to curfews. Consequently, Jews made up a significant proportion of the membership of urban and rural guerrilla groups operating in France, Italy, Belgium and Greece, although they constituted a tiny percentage of the population.

As early as September 1939, the Jews of Belgium, many of whom were refugees from Eastern Europe, had formed what is believed to have been the first Jewish resistance group outside the Reich. Others joined the active Zionist organizations Solidarité and Fraternal Aid, which advocated armed resistance and also provided documents and money to those in hiding or wishing to travel to neutral countries. In addition, they carried out isolated acts of sabotage including the derailment of German supply trains and the assassination of collaborators, including one of their own who had compiled lists of Jews for deportation.

There were also raids on the offices of the Judenrat (Jewish Council), which felt compelled to comply with German demands for lists of Jews for deportation. In the summer of 1942, a daylight raid on the Brussels office of the Judenrat secured lists that were to have been handed over to the Gestapo. The deportations continued, but several members of the Judenrat resigned when they realized they were being used by the Nazis. A leading member of Belgium's Judenrat was assassinated in the street in the hope of deterring others from working for the enemy.

That September, the welfare of Belgium's remaining 90,000 Jews became the responsibility of the Comité de Défense des Juifs (CDJ), which found sanctuary for 3,000 Jewish children with Belgian families and in children's homes with the assistance of the Church and charity organizations. The CDJ also facilitated the safe passage of 10,000 adults to neutral countries.

Belgian resistance

By the spring of 1942, there were three Jewish resistance units operating in Belgium, who had access to a rudimentary laboratory for manufacturing explosives and printing fake documents. Dozens more with no Jewish connection joined guerrilla groups in the Low Countries.

The links established between the Jewish and non-Jewish groups proved crucial when they needed to launch a joint operation, as happened on 19 April 1943. That day, the CDJ learned of a train transporting 1,500 Belgian Jews to Auschwitz only hours before it was due to leave.

Fortunately, they were able to co-ordinate an attack with the help of a group led by brothers George and Alexander Lifshitz, who were familiar with the route and knew of a remote rural location at Tirlemont in Flanders where it could be ambushed. They freed 700 men, women and children, although 20 were gunned down by German guards and 400 were quickly recaptured. However, more than 300 were saved from certain death. A number of the wounded were subsequently rescued from the local hospital and joined their friends and families in hiding in Brussels and in the countryside, where they were sheltered and looked after by the partisans.

Two female members of the Jewish resistance in the Warsaw ghetto who were arrested by the Germans.

FRANCE

French Jews committed to the establishment of a Jewish homeland in what was then Palestine formed the Armée Juive in January 1942, while those whose only concern was to fight for France joined either the First or Second Detachment of the communist Francs-Tireurs et Partisans-Main d'Œuvre Immigrée (FTP-MOI). Both detachments consisted mainly of French Jews. It was important for those members of the Armée Juive that the Germans saw they were fighting Jews; for that reason, they wore armbands to identify themselves. Though primarily a fighting unit, the Armée Juive also organized the evacuation of hundreds of Jews to safety in Spain and Switzerland.

Following the D-Day landings in June 1944, a number of these units joined forces to form the Organisation Juive de Combat (OJC). Under that name and wearing Star of David armbands, they fought to liberate Paris and other French cities. In their most audacious operation, they seized a German troop train and taunted their humiliated prisoners with cries of 'Ich bin Jude!'

A Parisian partisan

Polish refugee Abraham Lissner, a veteran of the Spanish civil war, returned to his adopted country of France and became a leader of the Jewish Partisan Unit of Paris. A fellow Pole, Leon Pakin, who had served with Lissner in the same all-Jewish guerrilla group in Spain, convinced him that they needed to form a new unit composed entirely of Jewish veterans of the Spanish war. This would ensure that they would not be betrayed by one of their own and that they would be fighting alongside men who could be trusted to watch their backs.

During the early months of the occupation, they were unable to obtain enough weapons to go around and so were reliant on their own resources and ingenuity. But within a few months, they found themselves under the command of the FTP (Francs-Tireurs et Partisans), the national resistance organization that allocated the missions and supplied the weapons and explosives. Lissner's group was one of four operating in Paris, each comprising men of the same nationality, the other units being Italian, Armenian and Romanian–Hungarian.

Each group was assigned a courier who provided the only link to their superiors. This was invariably a woman who could move more freely during the daytime without arousing suspicion. She brought them food, extra ration cards, weapons, ammunition and the bombs which for safety were assembled elsewhere and only needed to be primed.

Small victories

As isolated as they were, they were still vulnerable to infiltration by Gestapo agents and informers. For that reason, one of the group would be in contact with other resistance groups so that they could vouch for any potential new member who claimed to have worked with another group.

There was no guarantee that they could trust a new recruit. Even the most devoted patriot could turn informer under torture and the Gestapo had no qualms about threatening their families. For this reason, all resistance fighters were advised to avoid contact with their friends and families and assume a new identity. Under their new name, they would rent a room and establish a regular routine, so as not to arouse suspicion.

The FTP paid them just enough to live on, about 1,600 francs a month with 300 more for a married man with children, though family men were considered a greater security risk. Exceptions were made for those with particular skills, or who worked in a particular industry or factory with access to material or sensitive documents and passes that could be copied. It was also possible that a family man might be under less scrutiny, as it was not unknown for the Gestapo to put more than a dozen agents on to a single suspect so that if one were spotted, or lost contact with the target, another could take over.

Sometimes even the most careful resistance member could be caught by chance. Three women of the Jewish Partisan Unit in Paris were arrested in a routine police check and found to be carrying grenades. The police forced one to accompany them to her apartment, where they expected to find more explosives, weapons and incriminating documents. While they were searching, she jumped to her death from a window rather than be interrogated by the Gestapo. Her two companions were sent to Auschwitz and were never heard of again.

Lissner took an enormous risk to document the activities of his group that might never otherwise have been recorded, such as the bomb attacks on a German barracks, those on a café on the Place de la Concorde that was popular with German soldiers, and on a hotel in Montmartre frequented by German officers. Only rarely did his fellow Frenchmen and women hear of these small victories that had been won in their name by listening to the BBC and in the pages of the underground press.

Hit-and-run attacks

The pages of Lissner's diary for 1942–3 detail hundreds of missions in which he took an obvious pride, most notably the assassination of Dr Karl Ritter, the Nazi district leader responsible for the deportation of hundreds of thousands of Frenchmen to German slave labour camps.

Lissner also recorded numerous hit-and-run attacks by both his own group and what he called their 'immigrant allies' (the Romanian–Hungarian and Italian units). Together they were responsible for 29 bomb attacks on hotels frequented by German officers, 33 hand grenade attacks on similar targets, 15 arson attacks on Wehrmacht recruiting offices, 78 arson attacks on warehouses stockpiling war materials, as well as the bombing of 123 military buses and the spiking of two anti-aircraft batteries. In addition, there were assassinations of German officers and collaborators, as well as successful grenade attacks on groups of German soldiers and their barracks and numerous incidents of sabotage on the main railway network. In one derailment alone, 14 carloads of German weapons were destroyed and the line disrupted for several days.

In total, an estimated 3,000 German troops were killed in these attacks, which had a twofold purpose: that of demonstrating to the occupation forces that they were vulnerable and that they were considered legitimate targets, despite their threat of brutal disproportionate reprisals.

Sadly, Lissner and his Parisian comrades were ultimately betrayed by one of their own commanding officers who broke under torture. The group scattered and some were captured and executed. Lissner eluded the Gestapo and survived the war, but he was haunted to the end of his days by the sight of a poster he saw while on the run. It displayed his compatriots, the so-called 'Army of Criminals', their faces still bearing the bruises inflicted by their interrogators.

The forgotten Jews of the Algerian underground

José Aboulker had been the leader of the Algerian resistance, a movement composed almost entirely of Jews, so perhaps it was inevitable that his nephew, Max Danan, would join the Algerian Jewish Underground (AJU) during the German occupation of France.

There had been 800 volunteers, according to Jacques Zermati, a former commander of the AJU, 'but at the moment of truth, 400 of them had cold feet, and just 400 were left – almost all of them Jewish.'

Their part in the liberation of French North Africa has gone largely unnoticed by history, particularly French history, and Zermati suspects that this was due entirely to the anti-Semitic nature of the Vichy regime, which couldn't stomach the idea that it owed anything to French Jews and, moreover, French Algerian Jews.

Operation Torch, as the mission was known, was a combined Anglo-American landing designed to capture the Axis forces in a pincer movement and end the stalemate in North Africa that had seen the strategic port of Tobruk change hands several times over the course of the campaign.

Fortunately, many French army officers were anti-Vichy and sympathetic to the Free French government in exile under de Gaulle and so were willing to aid the underground. But the coastline of North Africa was defended by a formidable force of 50,000 French troops and their Axis allies – more than enough to repel a landing by a small force of untrained and poorly armed amateurs. Fortunately, they were able to substitute their men for key personnel at the command centre and to communicate by forging orders from a senior Vichy officer. Once their men were in place, they were able to countermand any orders to fire on the Allied Armada, which made an unopposed landing on 8 November 1942.

Marshal Pétain's deputy, General Alphonse Juin, found himself under arrest to the evident amusement of 400 Jewish partisans who would not have been permitted to look him in the eye on the streets of Vichy.

Jewish revolt in the ghettos

'I want people to know that there was resistance. Jews did not go like sheep to the slaughter. Many fought back – if there was the slightest opportunity – and thousands lost their lives fighting the enemy and working to save lives. I was a photographer. I have pictures. I have proof.'

Jewish partisan photographer, Faye Schulman

Contrary to popular belief, the Jews of Europe did not watch helplessly behind the walls and barbed wire of the ghettos while their fellow countrymen resisted their oppressors.

According to Gideon Hausner, chief prosecutor at the Eichmann trial, there was 'much organized and widespread resistance', despite the fact that the Jews were untrained, half-starved and had little in the way of arms, ammunition and explosives. Nevertheless, in almost every ghetto, slave labour camp and even in the concentration and extermination camps, the Jews organized themselves, planned escapes, acquired arms or made improvised weapons. The Warsaw ghetto is justly remembered as a modern Masada, a symbolic act of defiance in the face of Nazi genocide, but there were dozens of lesser-known armed revolts by Jews in the ghettos of Lithuania, Czechoslovakia and Russia.

Jewish partisans who had fled the ghettos to fight in the countryside derailed trains transporting fellow Jews to the extermination camps. Though the Germans killed many in the ensuing chaos and hunted down many more, hundreds were saved from the gas chambers in this way. Even inside the camps, there were isolated acts of sabotage and attempts to disrupt the machinery of genocide, for which courageous individuals willingly sacrificed their lives. The crematorium at Auschwitz was destroyed and photographic evidence of the camp's mass murder obtained and smuggled out to the Allies at great personal risk. At Sobibor and Treblinka, the brutalized, emaciated inmates organized successful revolts.

Others resisted by non-violent means, sharing their meagre rations and obtaining essential provisions to alleviate suffering and to ensure their survival, so that they could testify to their barbarous, inhuman treatment and see the guilty called to account for their crimes. Some acts of sabotage were merely symbolic, a reckless gesture of defiance, such as that enacted by Jewish tailors in the Warsaw ghetto, who stitched buttons on German uniforms the wrong way round and sewed trouser legs together in a batch of German uniforms. But even ultimately futile acts such as these restored their pride and proved that they were not the *Untermenschen*, the subhumans, that the Nazis believed them to be.

Jews underground

In every occupied country, Jews slipped through the net by virtue of their ingenuity, the selfless actions of others or sheer luck and lived a precarious existence underground using false identity papers. Hundreds more were active in the French underground or fighting with the partisans in the occupied countries. In Croatia, 1,600 Jews joined the partisans, some serving as doctors, nurses and even cooks, contributing whatever they could in the struggle against an iniquitous ideology. Romanian Jews prevented the Aryanization of Jewish urban homes and businesses by the dictator Ion Antonescu and in Belarus, an estimated 15,000 Jews joined the partisans, making them the largest numerical group of armed Jews in Eastern Europe. Not all Jews were welcome to fight alongside their neighbours, however. Ukrainian Jews had suffered decades of persecution condoned by the Catholic Church. Consequently, Ukrainian Jews could not trust the partisans to protect them and so fought alone against two enemies – the Germans and their own countrymen.

Europe's secret fighters

More than 200 guerrilla groups in Eastern Europe were led by Jews who kept their true identify secret because they feared betrayal by their own comrades.

Not all the Jewish resistance fighters fought on their home territory. Many who had emigrated to what was then Palestine returned to Europe to join the fight against fascism.

Hungarian poet Hannah Senesh enlisted in the British army in 1943 as a paratrooper and was dropped into occupied Yugoslavia to organize resistance activities and rescue Allied soldiers and airmen trapped behind enemy lines. But soon after returning to her own country she was captured, imprisoned and tortured. She was executed on 7 November 1944 without betraying her comrades.

Countless more worked tirelessly and courageously behind enemy lines in Nazi-occupied Europe and kept silent after the war – or were muzzled by the communist dictatorship, which denied acknowledgement to all but state-approved heroes and heroines.

In all, one and a half million Jews served in the Allied armed forces, contrary to the belief that the Jews went meekly and obediently to their deaths.

Assassination in Switzerland

The first shot fired in defiance of the Nazis was heard on 4 February 1936, when a 27-year-old Jewish student assassinated a prominent Swiss Nazi, Wilhelm Gustloff. Gustloff was intent on inciting his countrymen to adopt Hitler's racist policies in a country that prided itself on its neutrality; Croatian-born David Frankfurter was determined to silence him, even if it meant he would spend the rest of his life in prison. It could be argued that the assassination was an act of self-defence, for it ensured the safety of Switzerland's 20,000 Jews and it kept the Nazis out of neutral Switzerland. The regime could not afford to instigate a pogrom on the eve of the Berlin Olympics, which attracted the world's press, as well as many of Nazi Germany's influential 'friends' from America and elsewhere.

Jews in occupied Poland

The Poles suffered particularly badly at the hands of the Germans during the occupation, but Polish Jews suffered far more than their compatriots. Long before they were herded into ghettos and butchered en masse by the SS, the Jews of Poland were routinely brutalized by the ordinary soldiers of the Wehrmacht and their officers.

From the earliest days of the occupation, supposedly 'spontaneous' acts of abuse were a common sight in Warsaw, Krakow and other centres, where Orthodox Jews congregated. Hasidic Jewish men, easily recognizable in their long black coats, wide-brimmed hats and traditional ringlets or sidelocks, were frequently humiliated by having their beards sheared in public while their fellow citizens stood round and mocked them. Young Jewish boys were not only physically maltreated, but also sexually molested in forced labour camps by their guards and Jewish

Jewish student David Frankfurter (left) with his lawyer Dr Lifschitz at Bern railway station in Switzerland en route for Palestine after his release from prison in 1945. He assassinated the Swiss Nazi Wilhelm Gustloff in 1936.

girls were degraded in every conceivable way with no possibility of their abusers being brought to account.

A Krakow biology student, Marina Graf, recalled how the Germans would routinely round up young Jewish girls for the most demeaning duties, such as scrubbing the pans in a sanitorium for highly infectious TB patients with their bare hands.

Warsaw resident David Widowinsky witnessed the shameful treatment enacted on some young Jewish women by a group of German army officers, who forced themselves into their apartment and ordered them to strip naked at gunpoint so that they could conduct intimate body searches. For their further amusement, the men ordered their victims to climb on to a table and jump down while one of their tormentors told his companions, 'Maybe something will fall out. One never knows how deep the Jewish swindlers can hide their jewels.'

Fatal transactions

The Nazis were so pathologically averse to the very existence of the Jews that they would execute anyone who helped them, even if it was something as seemingly insignificant as selling a Jew a single egg. Martin Gilbert's monumental history of the Holocaust, *Never Again*, records countless incidents of this kind. Indeed, a Jewish mother in Sosnowiec was hanged for buying an egg from a Polish peasant to feed her starving child. According to witness Frieda Mazia, the peasant was also hanged and the two bodies left in the market square as a deterrent to those who might have softened their hearts, or seen a profit, in selling food to the Jews.

But the frequent executions, the random shootings and the beatings were only the most visible manifestation of Nazi persecution in the occupied countries.

Victims endured an unseen ordeal on a daily basis. Mothers of young children compelled to report for forced labour had to leave their children behind unattended and hungry. In the ghetto, the community organized classes to keep them occupied, but the stress of separation coupled with severe deprivation would have a traumatic and lasting impact on the survivors.

> There were hundreds of little kids crying and begging for bread in the streets, and singing this tragic song, like a nightmare. We

used to throw food down to them. Mother would take her little piece of bread and when nobody would see, she would throw it out of the window to the kids. You'd have your favourite kids, and then one day you'd see them dead in the street.

Before the winter of 1940, the persecution of Poland's Jews and that of the Jews in other occupied countries had become highly organized and was running to a strict timetable. This forced exodus or 'resettlement', as the Germans called it, had been structured and systematized. Over several months, rural communities that had survived pogroms and persecution for centuries were uprooted overnight and resettled in walled ghettos in the poorest parts of Poland's cities, with poor sanitation and lack of basic necessities.

Sophie's choice

The Nazi occupation of Europe brought misery beyond the merely physical aspects of starvation, deprivation, forced confinement and brutality. It also forced ordinary people to make impossible choices, the memory of which would torture them for the rest of their lives.

In the ghettos and camps, mothers were not always willing to sacrifice themselves for their children, though many did. There are accounts of life in the Łódź ghetto and in Auschwitz that describe mothers abandoning their young children on arrival. During the selection process some sought safety among the mass of anonymous women, knowing what would become of them if they remained with their child. Fear for their own lives overcame their natural instincts to protect their child and if they survived until they were liberated, they must have suffered anguish and remorse every day and night until the day they died.

Even when young Jewish girls and women from the ghettos attempted to disappear in the crowd, posing as Gentiles, the smallest slip could give them away. Holocaust historian Judith Tydor Baumel gives the example of a young Polish Jewess who habitually cut carrots thinly as she would have done when making *tzimmes*, a traditional dish of sweet carrot eaten on the Sabbath, until her Polish co-workers noticed and gave her away. Her fate is not known.

Even instinctive reactions could prove fatal. Jewish women practised screaming *'Jesus Maria!'* when they were confronted to avoid blurting out an involuntary phrase which would reveal their true faith.

Harold Werner – Herschel Zimmerman

The fate of Poland's three million Jews is particularly tragic, for it was in support of Poland that the Allies had gone to war, but they ultimately failed to protect its sovereignty, its independence and its people.

Generations of Polish Jews had endured persecution, much of it sanctioned by the state and the Church, which was openly antagonistic toward Jews and had condoned successive pogroms from the pulpit. Anti-Semitism was endemic in Eastern Europe, but the German occupation unleashed latent hostility and effectively authorized all violent acts against Jews by those who regarded them with suspicion or envy.

Polish partisan Harold Werner and his 16-year-old brother Moishe had first-hand experience of their neighbours' enmity. Even before the war, they had been beaten up by thugs in full view of a policeman who deliberately looked the other way rather than intervene. During the occupation, Harold was repeatedly pulled out of a bread line by German soldiers after his fellow Poles identified him as a Jew and thereby not entitled to his ration.

Werner (whose real name was Herschel Zimmerman) was forced to leave Warsaw and find a village where he would not be recognized. But wherever he went, he encountered the same mindless hostility. Unable or unwilling to pass himself off as a Gentile, he was dependent on the charity of local villagers for shelter and food. In Hola, a village to the east of the capital, the local farmers refused all entreaties for shelter. One informed him that in a neighbouring village, both the farmer and the Jew that he had sheltered were set upon by a mob and beaten to death.

Werner managed to contact other young Jewish men and women in the area who were willing to take their chances in the forest rather than risk being betrayed by their own countrymen. But this was not without risk. The bitter winter claimed a dozen who were frozen to death. Being unarmed, they were also prey to marauding Russian guerrillas who raped the women while their men stood by helplessly. Shortly after that ordeal, the local villagers surrounded their camp armed with clubs and pitchforks and marched them to Sosnowica, where they were shot by the Germans. Werner and two friends miraculously survived, having gone foraging for food just before the villagers arrived. Once they had recruited more men and scavenged sufficient arms and ammunition from more sympathetic Russians and from the bodies of dead Germans, they dealt with the informers and the leaders of the manhunt. From that day, they had no more to fear from the villagers.

Werner's guerrilla warfare

By the spring of 1943, Werner's guerrillas numbered some 120 men and women, though fewer than one in five were armed. Their only hope of inflicting sufficient damage on the occupying forces was to contact larger, better experienced and armed groups and combine forces. They heard of an encampment in Parczew forest where hundreds of Jewish families had taken refuge on a network of natural islands in the middle of a swamp. It was little better than a ghetto and infested by mosquitoes, but at least they deterred the Germans from encroaching. Unfortunately, the drought that summer drained the swamp sufficiently for the Germans to mount an attack. While the men were on a raid, the Germans massacred the old men, women and children.

Werner and his fellow fighters were not only engaged in a guerrilla war against the German military, but also in a campaign against what they saw as an inhumane ideology. For that reason, they risked their lives to target more than just military objectives. In a Nazi slave labour camp at Adampol, the Germans had forced young Jewish women into prostitution, serving their Ukrainian and Latvian guards in a camp brothel. Werner and his men made three raids on the camp and freed more than a hundred of the women and young girls before the Germans murdered the rest and closed the camp.

The Bielski brothers

Thanks largely to the 2008 film *Defiance* starring Daniel Craig and the bestselling book on which it was based, the part played by the Bielski brothers in opposing the Nazis in Poland during the Second World War is now recognized. The four Polish partisans provided sanctuary for more than 1,200 Polish Jews in the Naliboki forest in north-west Belarus. Among them was 14-year-old Jack Kagan, who lived and fought with the Bielski brothers after escaping from a Nazi prison camp. Kagan testified to the brothers' heroic actions:

> The brothers were heroes. They saved my life and so many others. Without them we would all have been killed. They were much more concerned with saving

Jews than with killing Nazis. They did not kill innocent people. They killed collaborators who had betrayed the Jews to the Nazis, and any Nazis who threatened their community. The killings were a deterrent aimed at those who thought of selling Jewish lives to the Germans for a sack of potatoes. It was war and they were protecting their people who had seen thousands of Jews, including their own families, murdered by the Nazis.

The brothers were able to remain undiscovered for so long because they had chosen their hiding place well and knew every inch of it. Naliboki forest was a vast and formidable natural stronghold, housing a crude but fully equipped hospital, a bakery, bath house and workshops for the repair of weapons and the manufacture of clothes, furniture and other necessary items that could not be bought and transported across country. The makeshift 'village' in the forest had to be entirely self-sufficient and transportable in case it was discovered by the Germans, who had informants everywhere, even among the partisans.

Kagan remembers that there was a feeling of belonging in the camp, a camaraderie which offset the pain of being separated from their families: 'We were unhappy because so many members of our families, including my mother and sister, had been massacred. But we were happy because we were free and we were fighting back.'

The 'Jewish Residential Quarter'

Ben Kamm was 19 years old when he was forced to decide whether to follow his four younger brothers into the ghetto in Muranów, Warsaw's slum district, or take his chances with the partisans in the surrounding countryside. He took one look at the little room that his grandparents, parents and siblings would have to share with three other families and decided to leave. He was a fighter by nature, having endured years of verbal abuse, bullying and beatings from local youths and anti-Semitic gangs and was not inclined to submit to the Germans' demand that all of the city's Jews abandon their homes for the ghetto. In October 1940, all 450,000 of Warsaw's Jews were herded into an area just over a mile (3 km) square and were isolated in what the Germans euphemistically called the 'Jewish Residential Quarter'. Here, they reduced them to starvation within sight of their former neighbours, who could do little to help them even if they were willing to risk imprisonment – or worse – to do so. Having imprisoned the Jews behind high walls ringed with barbed wire and topped with shards of broken glass, the Germans had effectively quarantined the faction of the population who the Nazi Propaganda Ministry had depicted as contagious vermin and a threat to the Aryan race. It was an image that many in the occupied countries had accepted, particularly those predisposed to be suspicious of a people and culture they considered 'alien'.

In a deliberate policy to reduce the Jewish population by starvation, the Germans determined they be reduced to living on 187 calories a day, a tenth of the minimal adult requirement. The resulting malnutrition would raise the likelihood of disease, which spread rapidly in the overcrowded warren that was the ghetto, leaving fewer Jews to transport to the extermination camps.

> 'Everywhere there was hunger, misery, the atrocious stench of decomposing bodies, the pitiful moans of dying children. Children, every bone in their skeletons showing through their taut skins, played in heaps and swarms. "They play before they die," I heard my companion on the left say, his voice breaking with emotion.'
>
> Jan Karski, *The Story Of A Secret State*, 1944

Kamm's escape

Soon, the citizens of Warsaw became indifferent to the sight of emaciated corpses in the street, where they had died begging for food. Like many Jews of his generation, Ben Kamm was prepared to risk all to save his family from a similar fate. Fortunately, his blond hair and blue eyes gave him a chance to pose as an Aryan and, as luck would have it, an aunt had married a Polish army officer and was living outside the ghetto. She provided her nephew with food parcels and offered to supply forged identity papers, which her son could print without fear of discovery as he owned a printing works.

Being young and impatient to strike back at the enemy, Kamm left the city to join the partisans, who were rumoured to be carrying out raids against the Germans near Lublin. He recruited nine young men and walked with them the 95 miles (153 km) to Lublin, not daring to board a train or hitch a ride for fear of being challenged and having his papers checked. Kamm recalls, 'We thought the war would be over in a couple of months. Russia and England and France are in the war, they're going to crush Hitler. So we didn't expect this, the war to last.'

The group was fortunate enough to make contact with a guerrilla unit led by a former Polish officer, Grzezor Korczynski, but even a man of Korczynski's experience could be fooled by informers. He made the mistake of trusting a local farmer, who betrayed them to the Polish police. In the ensuing gun battle, five of Ben's comrades were killed. Three others chose to return to the ghetto and take their chances.

They had had enough of living rough, scavenging for food and playing host to lice. Reluctantly, Kamm made the long trek back to Warsaw when he received news of German plans for the liquidation of the ghetto: 'I think that the human mind cannot comprehend what happened. That they were going to take people and gas them and kill them by the millions, it didn't even come into my mind.'

He rejoined his unit before the uprising but feared for his own life when Korczynski had 16 Polish soldiers – all of them Jews – shot for refusing to hand over their money, which the commander had claimed his group needed to buy provisions and weapons. He justified their deaths by claiming that their refusal meant that they were not willing to obey orders. Ben had his doubts:

> Because he killed Jews, I was angry. Eventually, he would have done it to me… I can't forgive people [who] killed innocent babies, innocent women, innocent people… They killed the best of us. I am just very sorry that more of our Jewish boys and girls did not have the opportunity to do the same as I did.

The Warsaw ghetto

The Warsaw ghetto was more than an open prison for Warsaw's 450,000 Jews. It was a symbol of Nazi oppression and their contempt for the Jews, who were compelled to pay for building the 10 foot (3 m) high wall, as well as for the petrol used to burn their synagogue on Stawki Street to the ground, on the pretext that it posed a 'health hazard'.

And yet the elders among the Jews repeatedly refused to approve plans for an uprising proposed by the young leaders of the Jewish Fighting Organization, the Jewish Bund (the Jewish Socialists), the Jewish Military Union and other various Zionist organizations, who disagreed in many aspects but were united in their opposition to passive compliance with the Germans. The old men believed that it would only enrage the Germans and endanger the women, children and the elderly.

Until the transportation of nearly 200 orphans to Treblinka on 6 August 1942, Adam Czerniaków, leader of the Jewish Council, hoped that the Germans would offer them a peaceful resettlement in the East, though there was ever reason to suspect this was a mere cover story, a smokescreen for what actually awaited them. Czerniaków subsequently committed suicide, prompting one of the resistance fighters to condemn him for not taking any Germans with him.

From that day, attitudes hardened. The ghetto's unofficial diarist, Emmanuel Ringelblum, wrote:

> We should have run into the street, set fire to everything in sight, have torn down the walls, and escaped to the Other Side. The Germans would have taken their revenge. It would have cost tens of thousands of lives, but not 300,000. Now we are ashamed of ourselves, disgraced in our own eyes, and in the eyes of the world, where our docility has earned us nothing. This must not be repeated now. We must put up a resistance, defend ourselves against the enemy, man and child.

The Jews of Warsaw retaliate

Only 60,000 Jews remained, but they now had no doubt that they would die. The question was only whether they would be permitted to die fighting or be butchered at the end of the line that led to Treblinka.

They were poorly armed, having been refused weapons by the Polish Home Army on the grounds that guns would be wasted on untrained fighters and that if the rising was successful, it might encourage further risings in other Polish ghettos, with catastrophic loss of life. Neither argument dissuaded the Jews of Warsaw from fighting back with home-made bombs, Molotov cocktails and crude, makeshift weapons. They had managed to obtain a dozen rifles and revolvers bought from Poles outside the wire and were confident they would soon accumulate more from the

Germans. Fearful though they were, they were also impatient to begin the battle.

The first shots were fired on 18 January 1943 as a response to German acts of brutality. Though it was no more than a skirmish, it was enough to see the Germans off and left the inhabitants of the ghetto euphoric. As one later commented, it had erased the 'shame of Jewish passivity'. It also convinced the Polish Home Army, the official resistance movement, to supply the ghetto fighters with grenades, explosives and guns, although some of the revolvers proved to be useless.

The battle for the ghetto

Preparations for the real battle for the ghetto did not begin until 16 February and it is clear that the Germans did not underestimate the tenacity or determination of their opponents, as SS Reichsführer Heinrich Himmler promised Hitler that the ghetto would be *Judenfrei* by the Fuhrer's 54th birthday on 20 April. In fact, the 'Jewish bandits', as Himmler called them, held the Germans off from 19 April until 16 May 1943, beating back repeated assaults with tanks, armoured vehicles, flamethrowers, two battalions of crack Waffen-SS troops, as well as units of regular soldiers, Polish police and more than 100 agents of the Gestapo.

In the end it was the remorseless artillery shelling which finally wore down the defenders. There were few buildings that could offer them cover. The ghetto had been systematically levelled until the remnants of the ghetto army were forced underground in the sewers and cellars, which the Germans flooded with poison gas and attacked with stick-bombs and flamethrowers. For weeks, the survivors lived in the ruins, with little fresh water and almost no food. Those in the underground bunkers were in perpetual darkness and desperately trying to keep the children as quiet as possible, for it was known that the Germans had brought in sensitive listening equipment. At least one infant was smothered because its persistent crying would have given away the hiding place of one group of survivors.

And all the while, the Poles went about their business on the other side of the wire, gathering in groups to watch the Jews 'frying' as one of them put it. During the Easter weekend, there had been a fair with a merry-go-round that played a cheerful tune while the crackling of rifle and machine gun fire could be heard just a few hundred yards away and Jews could be seen jumping from burning buildings to their deaths.

Beaten by the flames

Eventually the Polish underground were moved to offer assistance, firing on the Germans from positions outside the ghetto and smuggling 24 Jewish survivors out through the sewers. But the battle for the ghetto was already lost: 'We were beaten by the flames, not the Germans,' rued ghetto commander Marek Edelman.

Three hundred Germans are thought to have been killed and their all-out armoured assaults repulsed by poorly armed and largely untrained civilians, more significantly the '*Untermenschen*' so derided by the Master Race. The defenders of the Warsaw ghetto had known from the outset that their fight was always going to end in defeat; it was just a case of how long they held out for. They kept the Germans at bay for a month, longer than the Polish army had done in September 1939.

Polish-born Holocaust historian Israel Gutman, a survivor of the Warsaw ghetto uprising, told a gathering at a Holocaust Day memorial in 1998:

> When the uprising started, it was Passover eve. Homes in the ghetto, even though they knew their days were numbered, held a seder. Members of the Jewish Fighting Organization began going from house to house to let everyone know it was starting. The ghetto became a fighting city. The first German assault was pushed back and they left the ghetto. At least for a few hours the ghetto was liberated territory. We knew we had no chance of saving our lives ... but there was a sense of obligation, of duty to participate in the rising.

SS commander Jürgen Stroop boasted to Berlin that his men had exterminated 50,000 'Jewish bandits', but could not hide his disbelief at their will to fight on against insurmountable odds:

> The Jews surprised me and my officers [...] with their determination in battle. And believe me, as veterans of World War I and SS members, we knew what determination in battle was all about. The tenacity of your Warsaw Jews took us completely by surprise. That's the real reason the *Großaktion* lasted as long as it did.

Exulting in chaos, SS-Brigadeführer Jürgen Stroop (centre in a field cap) watches blocks of housing go up in flames during the Warsaw ghetto uprising, 1941.

An unexpected defiance

The Germans had not expected the Jews to resist. They had robbed them of their citizenship and their rights by passing increasingly restrictive laws and few had protested. Having excluded Jews from public and professional life, the Nazis made it illegal for Jews to marry or have intimate relations with Gentiles. Those who were already married were marginalized from society and categorized as being in a mixed marriage, their children branded *Mischlings* (of mixed race). And still few raised objections; those who did were ignored, beaten into silence or imprisoned.

The Nazis then stigmatized the Jews by demanding they wear a yellow Star of David in public and finally, they herded them into ghettos where they were forced to live in overcrowded, unsanitary conditions in preparation for their deportation to forced labour and concentration camps.

The Nazis believed that the Jews were a passive, cowardly race who could be tricked and cowed into compliance. They could not imagine their young men and women taking up arms as they did in Warsaw, holding off the formidable German troops for weeks with homemade bombs and precious little ammunition. But the Jews of Warsaw and their compatriots across occupied Europe knew they were doomed and saw no alternative but to fight back and die with dignity.

Tragically, for those among their friends and family members who had either believed the Nazi lie that they would be 'resettled' or sent to work camps in the East, and who had convinced themselves that the rumours of mass exterminations were unfounded, when they finally learned the truth, it was too late.

Częstochowa ghetto

In the spring of 1943, a number of determined members of the Częstochowa ghetto, which lay 150 miles (241 km) to the south-west of the capital, obtained a small cache of weapons and grenades from the Jewish Fighting Organization in the Warsaw ghetto. Although the Polish underground refused to arm the Jews of Warsaw, they shared what little they had with their fellow Jews in other ghettos. Despite having few weapons themselves, they could not refuse the Jews of Częstochowa who had reduced their pitiful rations even further in order to save money to buy guns. If they could not obtain arms, the Jews of Częstochowa were prepared to set fire to the ghetto and die together in a futile act of martyrdom.

They organized raids on German warehouses where confiscated goods were stored and obtained German uniforms so that they could move freely around the city by bribing unscrupulous members of the Wehrmacht, who would occasionally even sell them weapons, though doing business with Germans was extremely precarious.

Even inside the ghetto the Jews were not safe from harassment. The Germans would stage routine inspections, so the weapons workshops were dismantled every night, moved to a new location the next morning and reassembled, ready to repair the malfunctioning guns that had been sold to them by unscrupulous contacts. Poles were expressly forbidden to supply the inhabitants of the ghettos with food, clothing or anything that might sustain life. Those who may have felt a twinge of Christian compassion were deterred by signs posted outside the walls warning of the risk of contagious disease from contact with the inhabitants.

In June that year, the Częstochowa underground were so desperate to obtain more weapons that they were forced to trust a German truck driver, who subsequently betrayed them to the Gestapo. One member of the underground was killed, a second managed to escape while a third was captured and tortured in front of his fellow Jews in the ghetto. But he died without betraying his friends.

A few days later, on 25 June, the Germans launched a raid on the ghetto, firing indiscriminately and throwing grenades into groups of terrified civilians. The Jewish resistance fighters had made preparations to repel an attack, but were taken by surprise. They were killed before they could reach their underground arsenal. Only a few managed to flee through a network of tunnels leading out of the ghetto and hide in the surrounding countryside. Hundreds of men, women and children were murdered after being forced to march to the Jewish cemetery.

Vilna

'Let us not go like sheep to the slaughter, Jewish youth! Anyone who is taken out through the gates of the ghetto, will never return. All roads of the ghetto lead to Ponary, and Ponary means death...It is true that we are weak, lacking protection, but the only reply to a murderer is resistance. Brothers, it is better to die as free fighters than to live at the mercy of killers. Resist, resist, to our last breath.'

Abba Kovner, Vilna resistance leader, 1 January 1942

Thirty-five thousand of Vilna's Jews had been murdered by the Germans in 1941, leaving the survivors in little doubt as to what was being prepared for them if they didn't fight back. The younger occupants of the ghetto were impatient to strike at the enemy as soon as possible, though the consequences for breaking the 10 pm curfew were terrible.

In May 1942, three young men slipped out of the ghetto to plant a mine on the main railway line, derailing a troop train and killing 200 Germans. Weapons were seized from the dead and hidden in a nearby forest for use in future raids. But it wasn't until the following January that the Zionist and communist factions joined forces to form the Fareynkite Partizaner Organizatzye (FPO).

Although its members had no military training or experience, they were organized and highly disciplined. They were also well-equipped with a subterranean arsenal comprising 50 machine guns, 30 revolvers, dozens of grenades and thousands of rounds of ammunition obtained from a German ammunition factory. The underground also printed a regular newspaper, the *Flag of Freedom*, printed in a secret workshop outside the ghetto and distributed to the general population, as well as a Russian language pamphlet for Soviet POWs and a handwritten Yiddish language pamphlet for those inside the ghetto.

But the FPO lost the support of the community they had formed to protect when they refused to hand over their leader, Yitzhak Wittenberg, to the Gestapo in July 1943. The Germans threatened to liquidate the ghetto and murder the women and children if he was not handed over and so he had no choice but to give himself up. He died in custody the next day.

As a consequence of the so-called Wittenberg Affair, many men of the FPO left the comparative safety of the ghetto for the surrounding forest, where they were hunted down and killed by the Germans. Fewer than 20 survived. The Germans, however, were not satisfied and took revenge on the families of the men who had joined the Jewish resistance. They then surrounded the ghetto, which was defended by those resistance fighters who had decided to remain to protect the old men, women and children. These fighters put up such stiff resistance that the Germans were forced to agree to a ceasefire, during which 200 members of the resistance slipped out of the ghetto and took refuge in the Narocz and Rudnitska forests, where they vowed to continue the fight.

Supported by 200 Ukrainians, the Germans stormed the ghetto on 23 September and crushed the revolt. They executed the few remaining defenders and transported the inhabitants of the ghetto to the Vaivara concentration camp in Estonia. The able-bodied were taken to the Heereskraftpark labour camp.

Minsk

The Germans rarely entered the ghettos unless they were rounding up its inhabitants for transportation to concentration camps, extermination camps or slave labour camps. They could not, however, afford to leave the imprisoned populations unsupervised and so they delegated responsibility for the security of the ghetto to the Jewish police. These volunteers received extra rations in return and the assurance that they would be excluded from the round-ups. Although, in practice, it guaranteed nothing more than that they would be the last to be transported to the camps. The volunteers were despised by their former neighbours and friends, but their presence meant that it was possible for an underground movement to operate unmolested by the Germans, provided the Jewish police could be outwitted, bribed or persuaded to turn a blind eye.

By such means, the resistance in the Minsk ghetto were able to offer sanctuary and medical treatment to more than 20 wounded partisans in the summer of 1941. The men were also given forged papers and new identities. As soon as the wounded had recovered, they were to join the 10,000 Jewish partisans training and organizing resistance in Minsk – the largest number operating inside a ghetto in Eastern Europe. They were to have joined the Byelorussian partisans in the countryside, but the Germans had driven them back, too far to be contacted. The ghetto fighters then formed all-Jewish guerrilla units to carry out hit-and-run raids, derailing German troop and supply trains, attacking military convoys and cutting communications.

The Minsk guerrillas were also directly responsible for the assassination of Generalkommissar Wilhelm Kube in September 1943. Kube had been in command of the squad who murdered all of the children in the ghetto's children's home by burying them alive. While they screamed, he had thrown sweets into the pit. His assassination was a signal to the Nazis that there were those who would willingly sacrifice themselves to seek retribution for such atrocities. In this case, it was a woman who planted the bomb under the general's bed – namely, Kube's domestic servant, Halina Mazanik – as no Jewish male could have got near him.

The Nazis were forced to concede that they had seriously under-estimated the Jews who were, in the words of the Reichskommissar of Riga, 'far superior' in intelligence to the 'mass of the White Russian populace' and 'the driving force of the resistance movement'. The Reichskommissar's report, dated 20 November 1941, concluded that the Jews of Minsk were 'the originators and instigators and in most instances even the perpetrators' of the most effective acts of resistance.

Łachwa

Had the occupants of the ghettos been supplied with sufficient arms and ammunition, it is likely that the majority would have set aside any qualms they might have had regarding breaking the Sixth Commandment which prohibits the killing of another human being, for it would have been a simple matter of self-defence. Their concession to take up arms against their persecutors stemmed from the realization that without sufficient weapons and explosives, they stood no chance against overwhelming and superior forces. There were occasions when they had no choice but to sacrifice themselves to ensure that even a few of their number might survive.

On 3 August 1942, the 2,000 inhabitants of the Łachwa ghetto in south-west Byelorussia were told that the ghetto was to be razed to the ground and that they would be massacred – but not until their SS executioners had finished their meal. Himmler's elite were hungry and exhausted after killing tens of thousands of men, women and children in nearby Hohorodek and Luniniece. They would get around to the business of erasing Łachwa from the map when they were suitably rested and had eaten their fill.

If the Germans expected their victims to beg for mercy or beseech their God to deliver them, they were mistaken. The able-bodied snatched up whatever lethal implement came to hand and set upon their would-be killers. They were no match for the heavily armed SS who fired into the crowd, killing 1,400 before the butchery was done. But several of the SS wouldn't live to murder any more Jews and 600 of the ghetto's inhabitants took advantage of the confusion to flee into the surrounding forest. Nearly

400 of these were later hunted down and murdered, but more than 100 survived that spontaneous revolt to live and fight another day with the local partisans.

Tuczyn

A similar scene occurred at the Tuczyn ghetto in western Ukraine on 23 September 1942, when the Germans and their Ukrainian militia ordered the 3,000 occupants to assemble for transportation to labour camps. Refugees from elsewhere in the region had recently arrived in the ghetto and had warned the occupants what would happen if they complied with the orders. In a mass break-out, 2,000 breached the perimeter fence and fought a fierce battle, using improvised weapons as well as the guns and grenades they had been stockpiling in anticipation of the round-up. Dozens of German and Ukrainian soldiers were killed, with many more seriously wounded, but 1,000 Jewish civilians were also killed.

Of the 2,000 who fled to safety, 400 were soon tracked down and persuaded to return to the ghetto with promises that they would not be ill-treated. They were summarily executed, as were another 150 who surrendered after braving hunger and the bitter winter.

Białystok

On 15 August 1943, the leader of the Judenrat in Białystok in north-eastern Poland was informed that the 40,000 inhabitants of the ghetto were to be transported to Lublin the following day as they were no longer of 'economic value' to the Reich. It was the news they had dreaded since August 1941, when 50,000 of the region's Jewish population were herded into the ghetto under armed guard, but it was also the signal for action for which they had been waiting impatiently for two agonizing years.

They were the survivors of the massacres that had followed the German occupation of the city on 27 June 1941, when 2,000 had been shot dead in the streets and hundreds more burned alive in the main synagogue. A week later, 200 more had been butchered in the fields outside the city and another 5,000 were murdered on the same site that July. Two months later, 4,000 had been transported to the Pruzany ghetto and from there to Auschwitz in January 1943.

It is likely that not one of Białystok's Jewish inhabitants would have been left to testify to what had taken place that summer had they not been useful to the new Aryan owners of the factories and workshops supplying the SS and the Wehrmacht on the Eastern Front.

Now the hour of reckoning was near, they feared what would follow if they were to break out and attempt to link up with the Polish underground in the forests to the west or the Soviet partisans operating to the east, north and south. The Poles were known to shoot Jews on sight and the Russians were an unknown factor – possibly sympathetic, but just as likely to turn on them as the Poles. If, by a miracle, they repelled the Germans and made a break for the countryside, they could be running into a trap set by their 'natural' enemies.

Under the collective banner of the 'Anti-Fascist Fighting Bloc' the various groups inside the ghetto set their differences aside and pooled their meagre resources.

These amounted to two dozen rifles, one heavy machine gun, several sub-machine guns and a hundred handguns, many of them bought or bartered for from the Polish peasants who had scavenged for guns after the rout of the Polish army four years earlier. Predictably, the guns had not been looked after and would seize after firing a round or two. It was a pitiful arsenal to arm 500 men and women of the resistance who were preparing to fight for their lives and who could do nothing but pray for deliverance.

That morning, they issued a call to arms: 'Five million European Jews have already been murdered by Hitler and his executioners... Each of us is under a sentence of death. We have nothing to lose!... Let us not behave like sheep going to the slaughter!'

Dispatching the expendable

The Germans were determined that Białystok would not prove to be another Warsaw and sent in three battalions supported by armoured cars, artillery and tanks. Two of those battalions were Ukrainians, whom the Germans considered expendable. If they were repulsed, the local commander could blame the lack of courage displayed by his Ukrainian allies. But the Ukrainians were merciless. They mowed down the women and children who had formed a barrier to protect the fighters, who had been corralled into three narrow streets backing on to the perimeter fence. For six days, the poorly armed ghetto guerrillas kept the Ukrainians and Germans at bay, but finally resorted to setting the ghetto ablaze in the hope of escaping through the smoke.

It was not lack of courage but lack of weapons and ammunition that finally defeated them. Had they possessed a fraction of the arms supplied to the Polish Home Army by the British, they might have made the enemy pay dearly for their crimes.

AFTERWORD

Hitler's febrile vision of a world ruled by one nation and by force was fated to fail. His Third Reich did not last a thousand years. It barely lasted twelve. And in that time, entire nations were forced into a life-and-death struggle with a ruthless totalitarian regime and its equally unprincipled allies. Towns, cities and villages across Europe were reduced to rubble, communities uprooted, entire cultures eradicated and countless innocents condemned to death, brutalized or imprisoned on the merest suspicion of opposing this most repressive of regimes.

It is estimated that between 70 and 85 million people died in the Second World War, the majority of them civilians, of whom between 48 and 63 million perished primarily as a consequence of the indiscriminate bombing of densely populated areas. Millions more were murdered as a result of systematic genocide, hundreds of thousands were tortured and an untold number were butchered in sadistic experiments carried out in the name of a spurious, perverted science.

Hitler's Germany was a gangster state that attracted the criminal and corrupt, the bitter failures and the incompetent, as well as the highly educated and intelligent, who saw in it the means by which they could exercise influence and enrich themselves at the expense of others. It was all about will – *Triumph of the Will* – to borrow the title of Leni Riefenstahl's 1935 Nazi propaganda film: Hitler's all-conquering self-belief that, despite his many flaws and failings, he would rise to the top of the heap and raise his wild-eyed, fanatical acolytes with him to the summit. From there, they would look down on the mass of festering,

Hitler poses beside a Mercedes during the Nuremberg Rally, 1934; in the foreground is film director Leni Riefenstahl, who is shooting Triumph of the Will.

pitiful humanity like the Gods of Olympus and gloat. At one point it looked as if they might see their lurid vision come true.

The Third Reich won swift victories in the first three years of the war by means of its military might, the shock tactics of the blitzkrieg and the unpreparedness that immobilized and fatally undermined its adversaries. But once its opponents had capitulated, it was evident that there was no coherent plan, no unifying vision, no consensus on how to exploit what Germany had seized by force, threats and intimidation. When asked by his foreign office functionaries for a statement regarding his political programme for the future, Hitler replied that 'no preparations for peace are necessary'. There was no leadership or direction from the Führer regarding the future of the conquered countries, nor even of those who had joined the Axis, or offered to collaborate in return for territory lost at the end of the First World War or the empty promise of peaceful coexistence. Hitler had no sense nor understanding of his conquests' national interests and even less inclination to govern them once he had seized what he coveted. He was an indolent man and a turbulent personality, a demagogue, whose only interest lay in conquering and subjugating his enemies, plundering their treasures and resources, and, having done so, losing interest altogether.

Contrary to the image portrayed in Nazi propaganda, Nazi Germany was not a unified and highly disciplined regime, but a chaotic hive of conflicting interests and bitter rivalries, both within the hierarchy and at the lowest levels between the Party's bosses and bureaucrats. The SS and the army loathed and distrusted each other, various ministries and institutions were ideologically and politically opposed and the aberrant individuals within the administration were engaged in a constant and vicious struggle to win the favour of their Führer. This frenzied enmity, competitiveness and suspicion was projected on to the subordinated states, where the administration was largely improvised and unsystematic. As Vichy premier Pierre Laval remarked when he was accused of having served an authoritarian state – 'Yes, and what a lot of authorities.'

The Nazi leadership was blinded by their pathological obsession with race. This would lead them to treat the occupied countries differently depending upon their racial demographic and this inconsistency and irrational approach would reveal what one commentator referred to as their 'political incompetence'. The Nordic nations would be coaxed and cajoled into co-operating in the hope that they would come to see themselves as Aryan brothers to the self-styled 'Master Race', while the

Slavs to the east would be enslaved and their lands colonized by German settlers. But this approach failed abysmally. When the Danes were permitted to hold free elections in 1943, the Nazis won only two per cent of the vote. Whether the Nazis permitted the civil administration a certain freedom, as they did in Denmark, or attempted to control every aspect of life with threats and violence, as they did in Czechoslovakia, they failed to silence the opposition. The underground press and armed resistance movements flourished in every occupied country, although the extent of their activities varied depending on how effective the Nazi terror apparatus was in crushing dissent.

More than 70 years after the end of the Second World War and the defeat of Nazi Germany, there is little remaining of Hitler's Thousand Year Reich. Even the massive arena at Nuremberg where the Nazis' 1930s rallies were staged is crumbling, having been shoddily built on unstable foundations from poor quality materials. What remains across Europe, in Germany and throughout their formerly occupied territories, are monuments to the Führer's hubris and hatred, such as the Topography of Terror in Berlin (a permanent exhibition on the site of what was the Gestapo's headquarters) and the Anne Frank House in Amsterdam. These exist alongside many other important museums and monuments to the Holocaust and the resistance, including the concentration camps whose preservation as museums serves not only as a remembrance – but a warning.

ONLINE AND ACADEMIC RESOURCES

Chapter 1

Michaela Raggam-Blesch (2019) '"Privileged" under Nazi-Rule: The Fate of Three Intermarried Families in Vienna', *Journal of Genocide Research*, 21(3), 378–397, DOI: 10.1080/14623528.2019.1634908

Visual History Archive, USC Shoah Foundation (2019) <https://sfi.usc.edu/vha>

Documentation Centre of Austrian Resistance (DÖW) (2019) <http://www.doew.at>

Private Prague Guide (2019) <https://www.private-prague-guide.com>

Chapter 2

Quora (2019) <https://quora.com>

Polish Greatness.Com (2017) <https://polishgreatness.com>

Nicholas Lane (1997) 'Tourism in Nazi-occupied Poland: Baedeker's *Generalgouvernement*', *East European Jewish Affairs*, 27:1, 45–56, DOI: 10.1080/13501679708577840

Global Nonviolent Action Database (2019) <http://nvdatabase.swarthmore.edu>

War History Online (2019) <https://www.warhistoryonline.com>

Loni Klara (2016) 'During the Nazi Occupation of Norway, Humor was the Secret Weapon' < https://www.atlasobscura.com/articles/during-the-nazi-occupation-of-norway-humor-was-the-secret-weapon>

The *Saturday Evening Post* (1943) < https://www.saturdayeveningpost.com/issues/?issue-year=1943>

National Museum of Denmark (2019) <https://en.natmus.dk>

Bjørn Schreiber Pedersen & Adam Holm (1998) 'Restraining excesses: Resistance and counter-resistance in nazi-occupied Denmark 1940–1945', *Terrorism and Political Violence*, 10(1), 60-89, DOI: 10.1080/09546559808427444

Chapter 3

Tom Holloway (2009) <http://timewitnesses.org>

Joshua Scott (n.d.) <memoirsofwwii.com>

BBC (2014) <http://www.bbc.co.uk/history/ww2peopleswar>

History News Network (2019) <http://historynewsnetwork.org>

Linda M. Woolf (1999) 'Survival and Resistance: The Netherlands Under Nazi Occupation' <http://faculty.webster.edu/woolflm/netherlands.html>

Anne Frank Fonds (2019) <https://www.annefrank.ch/de>

Marcel Ophüls (1969) *Le chagrin et la pitié (The Sorrow and the Pity)*

Simon Kitson (2002) 'From Enthusiasm to Disenchantment: The French Police and the Vichy Regime, 1940–1944', *Contemporary European History*, 11(3), 371–390 DOI:10.1017/S0960777302003028

Paul McQueen (n.d.) < https://theculturetrip.com/authors/paul-mcqueen>

Daily Express

Richard Bond (2002) *Hitler's Britain* Alliance Atlantic presentation of a Lion Television and AAC Fact production in association with Channel 5 and History Television and PBS

Chapter 4

Fabrice Virgili (2005) 'Enfants de Boches: The War Children of France', CNRS, Paris

CEGESOMA Centre for Historical Research and Documentation on War and Contemporary Society (2015) < http://www.cegesoma.be/cms/index_en.php>

Sarah Van Ruyskensvelde (2013) 'Remembering wartime schooling... Catholic education, teacher memory and World War II in Belgium', *Paedagogica Historica*, 49(1), 149–159, DOI: 10.1080/00309230.2012.744064

Chapter 5

István Rév (2018), 'Liberty Square, Budapest: How Hungary Won the Second World War', *Journal of Genocide Research*, 20(4), 607-623, DOI: 10.1080/14623528.2018.1522820

Kadar, Vagi and Ungvary, *Robbing The Corpses*, unpublished manuscript, 2003

Thomas Orszag-Land, 'A Fresh Look At Budapest's Holocaust'

Jane Gabriel (1986) *Greece: The Hidden War*, Channel 4 1986

Greek News Agenda (2015) <greeknewsagenda.gr>

Chapter 6

Lower, Wendy, *Nazi Empire-Building and the Holocaust in the Ukraine*, University of North Carolina, 2005

Chapter 7

Oral History Association (2000) *The Oral History Review*, 27(1), Oxford University Press

BIBLIOGRAPHY

Mark, Ber, 'The Warsaw Ghetto Uprising', in *They Fought Back: The Story of the Jewish Resistance in Nazi Europe*, ed. Yuri Suhl, N.Y. Paperback Library, 1968.

Fletcher, Willard Allen (ed.) *Defiant Diplomat George Platt Waller: American Consul in Nazi-Occupied Luxembourg, 1939–1941*, Rowman and Littlefield, 2014.

Fritzsche, Peter, *An Iron Wind: Europe Under Hitler*, Basic Books, 2016.

Karski, Jan, *Story of a Secret State: My Report to the World*, first published 1944.

Kirk, Tim, 'Workers and Nazis In Hitler's Homeland', in *History Today*, issue 7, July 1996.

Lemkin, Raphael, *Axis Rule in Occupied Europe: Laws of Occupation, Analysis of Government, Proposals for Redress*, first published 1944.

Mazower, Mark, *Hitler's Empire: How the Nazis Ruled Europe*, Penguin, 2009.

Morgan, Philip, *Hitler's Collaborators*, Oxford University Press, 2018.

Ottley, Roi, *No Green Pastures*, Charles Scribner's Sons, 1951.

Ringelblum, Emmanuel, *Notes from the Warsaw Ghetto: The Journal of Emmanual Ringelblum* ed. and transl., Jacob Solan, N.Y. Schoken Books, 1958.

Roland, Paul, *The Jewish Resistance*, Arcturus, 2018.

Rothchild, Sylvia, *Voices From the Holocaust*, New American Library, 1981.

Rousso, Henry, *Les années noires: Vivre sous l'Occupation*, Gallimard, 1992.

Sartre, Jean-Paul, *The Atlantic, December 1944/The Aftermath of War*, transl. Chris Turner, Seagull Books, 2008.

Time magazine, 26 March 1938.

Vinen, Richard, *The Unfree French: Life Under the Occupation*, Penguin, 2007.

Warring, Anette (ed.), *Surviving Hitler and Mussolini: Daily Life in Occupied Europe*, Berg, 2006.

Wouters, Nico, *Mayoral Collaboration Under Nazi Occupation in Belgium, the Netherlands and France, 1938–46*, Palgrave Macmillan, 2016.

INDEX

PICTURE CREDITS

All Images – Getty Images